The Mustard Seed

The Mustard Seed

Jackie Ellermann

authorHOUSE®

AuthorHouse™
1663 Liberty Drive
Bloomington, IN 47403
www.authorhouse.com
Phone: 1-800-839-8640

First published by AuthorHouse   9/14/2011

ISBN: 978-1-4670-3630-6 (sc)
ISBN: 978-1-4670-3629-0 (ebk)

Library of Congress Control Number: 2011916841

Printed in the United States of America

Any people depicted in stock imagery provided by Thinkstock are models, and such images are being used for illustrative purposes only. Certain stock imagery © Thinkstock.

Contents

*For our "family" at livercirrhosissupport
@yahoo groups.com
May God bless and watch over each
Precious life*

*And very special thanks to
Organ Donors Everywhere*

I tell you the truth, if you have faith as small as a mustard seed, you can say to this mountain, 'Move from here to there' and it will move. Nothing will be impossible for you." Matthew 17:20 NIV

Foreward

For over 18 years I have had the privilege of being pastor to Jackie Ellermann and her family. After moving to the Lehigh Valley from New Jersey, her first attraction to Trinity Wesleyan Church in Allentown, PA was the passion musicals presented during Easter weekend. The enthusiasm she brought to that ministry was encouraging and provided her entire family with the opportunity to connect with other ministries such as Live Nativity, traffic and parking, ushering, greeting, visitation and communion. She served the church for many years as Librarian. Jackie enjoys reading, and would often provide useful articles as resource on sermon topics.

This book, "The Mustard Seed" is a wonderful journey of faith during a most difficult time for the Ellermann family. While her beloved husband, John is loyal and devoted to his God, marriage, family and the church, these pages reveal the challenges that each family member rose to the occasion to confront. In the face of incredibly difficult odds, I can say without question that Jackie became the focused overcomer. Her coaching, determination and dedication was unmatched by anyone I have ever known. When most would become discouraged, Jackie plunged ahead with confidence that God would meet her family's needs according to His riches and glory. It didn't matter whether or not the hospital or doctors agreed. Jackie knew if God is for us, who would dare to stand against us.

As we have personally witnessed the faith of only a mustard seed that was able to move a mountain, even Jesus agreed that it doesn't take much when God is in it.

I am pleased to know the Ellermann family and consider them my dear friends. It is my profound prayer that this book will bring added encouragement to your life in whatever challenge you face. Jackie and John are a genuine example in the twenty first century that God's grace is sufficient. (Pastor Doug Heckman, Bridgeton Wesleyan Church)

Prologue

I am John, the primary subject of this book and would like to give you some background information before you begin reading it.

I was once told many years ago, *"You have a rough and rugged road to travel, beset with dangers . . . and may lose your life, an instance of the kind being on record."* (Masonic ritual) Well, I didn't lose my life through perilous times and dangers, but almost did.

This is the story of an amazing journey, written by an amazing person, my soul mate, my wife, that didn't begin with the idea of writing a book, but from the taking of notes, asking many, many questions, and discovering new information along the way.

Its original purpose was to be reminded of the details of the progression of a deadly disease and note the changes in it, for the doctors and medical staff who worked with us night and day. It is a reflection of her daily journaling. If you happen to know of, or be a caregiver to someone who is chronically ill, you may find this book to be very useful.

Reader, you are encouraged to make a cup of coffee or tea, prop up your feet and get comfortable. Read this sometimes graphic, explicit story of this long journey based on faith and courage. I hope you enjoy reading it as much as she did in writing it!

Anticipating The Future

"I, Jackie, take you, John to be my husband, and in doing so pledge to share my life with you. Encompassing all sorrows and joys, all hardships and triumphs, all the experiences of life. A commitment made in love, kept in faith, lived in hope and eternally made new."

Those were the words I spoke to my husband on October 1st, 1977 with family, friends, acquaintances, and co-workers looking on with great joy and admiration in their hearts.

I had met John on March 11, 1973 when I began working at Chas. F. Connolly Distributing Co., a local wholesale distributor of heating, air conditioning and related controls. John was a sales representative in the industrial controls dept.; I did clerical work.

My first few weeks at Connolly were spent helping John organize the filing system in his department, a task I found pleasant. I felt at ease with his blue eyes, ever-present smile and polite demeanor. We chatted aimlessly and became efficient co-workers together. Over the next two years I became more and more skilled at my job and helped anyone else in the company who needed help, proudly earning the title of Connolly's official "gal Friday."

These were the most delightful and congenial people I had ever worked for in my short career and I knew I had found a home here. They were like family and all seemed to care about each other.

Their compassion and concern became more evident as John's first marriage ended when his wife took their two small sons and re-located to Montana where she had spent her growing up years.

We all wondered that Saturday morning in September as we boarded the bus for the annual company picnic. 'Where is John?' It wasn't like John to say he planned to attend and then simply not show up. One of the men went inside and called John, then came back out and told us that John was experiencing some problems at home. We had all assumed that something unexpected must have happened. In fact, John's little family had left for Montana that previous night leaving John alone and devastated.

My co-workers and I felt bad for John. Upon his return to work the following weeks we continued our casual friendship. He would often ask my advice in life's dilemmas as co-workers sometimes do. Never in my life did I dream that this casual friendship would over the course of the years develop to the point of becoming best friends, soul mates and now husband and wife. Here we stood on our wedding day amid happy anticipation as we made a promise that would turn out to be a test of the vows spoken and a most difficult challenge of our journey through life's ups and downs.

The Happy Years . . .
And Then

Our years of happiness continued as we built our life together, completing our family with the birth of twin sons in 1981 and eventually settling in Allentown, PA. where John was offered a good position in industrial sales.

April 5, 2004: John is enjoying retirement, and at the prompting of our family doctor agreed to have a nuclear cardiac stress test. I dropped him off at the hospital and continued on my way to my part time job as a secretary for a local realtor whose office was a few blocks away. The stress test would take 4 hours. I would finish the day's work, pick John up and we would go home, have a nice nap and then maybe go out to dinner. We make our plans, but how quickly, in the blink of an eye, things change.

An hour later my world turned upside down. John called me and told me that he was being admitted to the hospital for further evaluation of blocked arteries. I was stunned and immediately drove the few blocks back to the hospital. The doctors told us they wanted to transfer him to the St. Luke's heart care unit in their Fountain Hill campus, a state of the art facility. I told them I knew where that was and offered to take him there right away. They said he would need to go by ambulance. By ambulance? Yikes! He had never ridden in an ambulance—ever!

Four days later on April 9th he underwent 4 way bypass surgery to clear the blockages to his heart. He had 95% blockage in 2 of his arteries and 90% in another 2, a heart attack waiting to happen.

We met some wonderful doctors who explained the procedure to us and gave us some literature to read. I immediately went to work reading the information so I could understand all that was about to happen and ask appropriate questions about what I didn't understand. The doctors were very willing to give me a "crash course" and made everything sound relatively simple. They would take a vein from John's leg, cut it into 4 pieces and simply attach it to his heart, forming a new route for his blood to circulate. It would take 4 hours and they do this procedure twice a day. Would we like morning or afternoon? It sounded like they were fixing a few hoses under the hood of a car so that it could move faster on a crowded freeway.

At the time, I thought 'this is the scariest thing that will ever happen to us' but I was to be proven wrong. John came through the surgery just fine and made a good recovery. Soon things were back to normal and we were living life, watching his diet, controlling his blood sugar and keeping his appointments for the routine blood work that revealed an enlarged liver and spleen. We were assured there was nothing to worry about, as his liver function tests were only slightly elevated.

Esophageal Varices

July 29, 2007: John's mom had passed away on December 14, 2006. John was in charge of taking care of her estate, which included selling the house she had owned for 50 plus years. We had much to do to prepare the house for sale, and a small window of opportunity to do so. The house was located in a beach resort community and Spring would be here before we knew it, followed by beach weather. At two blocks from the ocean the house would draw a hefty sum which would be divided between John and his two sisters.

We had found a buyer for the house. The closing would take place on July 31st. The buyers were scheduled to have their "walk through" on the 30th to make sure all repairs were done and everything was in order. John and I had decided to make the trip to the house the day before to make sure there would be no "surprises" when the prospective buyers did their walk through. We found a bulge in the kitchen wall looking as if water was building up inside the wall. The source of the leak was from the bathroom vanity above the kitchen. A plumber had been called in to make some repairs a week ago and it seemed something had gone wrong during his repair. We called him back and the problem was promptly corrected. We finished with the last of the "touch ups" that needed to be done and said our goodbyes to the house where John and his sisters had spent their summers as children growing up. There were many happy memories here, and we prayed that the buyers would enjoy their new home as much as John's family did.

We went to John's niece's house nearby for lunch before making the trip back home. Antoinette, who we lovingly call Ant, was in her mid 30's. She is John's sister, Lois' oldest daughter, and is a former deli manager at the local "Shop & Bag", a popular convenience store. Ant is a very good cook and has a real flare for catering. She had catered a party that we had for John in July of 2004, a few months after his heart surgery. John's birthday is Christmas Eve, so we decided to make it "Christmas Eve in July."

Ant, being disabled was not able to help us physically with the daunting task of emptying and fixing up the house for sale, but one thing she could do was make delicious meals for us after a day of hard work.

John was full after ½ of a BLT sandwich and said he was very tired. Two days prior, he had said he felt full with everything he ate. We thought nothing of it and attributed it to the stress of settling his mother's estate.

I took the wheel and drove home as John was understandably tired. He fell asleep by the time we were down at the end of Ant's block and slept all the way home.

Once we were home and rested we made our way over to church. It was a Saturday night and John wanted to prepare the baptismal tub for tomorrow morning's service. There were 6 people who would be baptized that morning. The tub needed to be positioned, filled and heated. The heating process took the longest. A small electric heater was placed into the filled tub and left there to do its duty for the remainder of the night in hopes that the chill would be gone from the water by 10:30AM on Sunday.

We were pretty tired once we were finished with all of this activity. When we arrived home at 9:30PM the backyard pool looked very inviting. We quickly put on our swimsuits and took a nice cool dip in the pool. It felt like the perfect ending to a long, hard day. We huddled together underwater and I asked John to promise me that we would always be together and that nothing would ever happen to separate us from each other. My dream was for us to enjoy many more moments together. Once his mom's house was sold we would be financially secure enough for me to retire from my job. This would give us lots of time to do the things we have always wanted to do, spending moments together that would grow into hours, days and even years.

But fate would have it that there would be many twists and turns on that road to retirement. We came in from the pool, dried off and put on our pajamas. John was very tired and wanted to go to sleep. I wondered why, since he had slept all the way home from his mom's house and then took a nap when we had arrived at home. Let's face it; it had been a long day.

I decided to stay up, watch TV and wait for our son, John to come home. Sometimes he stayed out late on Saturday, but he was never one to get into any trouble. I guess it's just my motherly instinct to make sure everyone is accounted for before I go to bed.

I was sitting in the living room watching Mel Brooks' "Young Frankenstein", one of John's favorite movies. I was delighted to hear him get up and make his way into the living room just in time for the good part where Gene Wilder was tap dancing with the monster. I started to say to him "look what's on" when he shuffled over to me and asked if I thought he felt warm. He did. I put my hand on his shirt and it was soaking wet from him sweating. He said he needed to get to the bathroom and felt like he needed to throw up. I remember thinking 'so this is it! He's having a heart attack!' At that point he began throwing up blood, lots of blood. This was no heart attack! Our son, Jimmy woke up and I told him to stay with his dad while I ran through the house to turn off that unnerving noise on the TV and retrieve the phone. John didn't want me to call 911 but I did anyway. It felt like I was outside myself watching a horror movie on TV. The bathroom certainly looked like a scene from a horror movie. There was blood everywhere!

I dialed 911 and said to the operator in the calmest voice I could muster, "My name is Jackie Ellermann." I gave my address and told them, "My husband is throwing up blood. Please come quickly." Then I repeated my name, spelling the last name and repeating the address. I can still remember how calm I sounded. I was very fearful that the dispatcher on the other end of the phone would get some small detail mixed up and the ambulance crew might take longer to find us.

Thank God they came quickly. I rode with John in the ambulance. Jimmy followed behind in his pick up truck. The ambulance driver took the 'scenic route'. At 3AM? I was beginning to think that I should have brought John there myself. We would have been at the hospital by now had I been driving.

Once we arrived at the emergency room John continued to throw up more blood. The doctors thought that perhaps he had an ulcer in his stomach but wouldn't be able to tell for certain until they could see into his stomach by using an endoscope with a camera on the end. An ulcer sounded like a possibility to me. After all, look what we had been through in the past handful of months! First they needed to remove all the contents of his stomach. They gave him 4 pints of blood to replace what he had lost and admitted him to the intensive care unit. I wanted to stay with him but the nurses assured me that he would be carefully monitored and they would call me at the first sign of anything unusual.

Jimmy drove me home at 5AM. He went to sleep and I cleaned up the blood in the bathroom. Then I curled up in a ball on my bed and tried to sleep for an hour before I would be allowed back into the hospital to stay with John. I couldn't sleep, and I was too scared to cry. It was time to be brave. I had no idea just how brave I would need to be in the future.

John was happy to see me when I showed up at the hospital. I pulled up a comfortable chair as close to the bed as I could. We were both so tired. I was able to rest my head on the pillow next to him while still reclined in the chair. We both fell asleep until I heard a nurse come in and remark to a 2nd nurse, "Aw! Look at the honeymooners." We would wait until around 3PM when John would have a procedure done to see where the bleeding was coming from. The good news was that the bleeding had stopped for the time being.

Our pastor came to visit us and we enjoyed some fellowship and prayer together. Pastor Doug is a great comfort to us. He had been our pastor ever since we had moved here to PA some 15 years ago. An excellent teacher, preacher, counselor and prayer warrior, he is truly a man of God.

Soon thereafter we met Dr. Cornell who would do the procedure. The nurses told me I could wait in the hallway, as they would require extra space in the room for the equipment needed for the test. The test would take about ½ hour. I made my way to the hallway where I could still see through a narrow window in the doorway directly into the room where John was. I said goodbye to Pastor Doug and began talking with two other women who were waiting to visit someone in the same unit. One of the women looked through the small window and said "Something must be going on in there!" Nurses and technicians were literally running through the hallways toward John's room. I saw his body convulse twice and saw someone pressing on his chest. Another technician was squeezing a blue air bag forcing air into his lungs. One of the nurses saw us looking in the window. She came to the doorway and told us we would have to leave the area. The other two women left while I stood there quietly and said "That's my husband. What's wrong?" "Oh! My God!" She answered. "I'll send the doctor right out."

Dr. Cornell came through the door attempting to look calm and controlled. How would he explain this to me? He told me that John wasn't breathing the way they wanted him to. The 'think bubble' over my head read 'he wasn't breathing at all' but I said nothing and waited for further explanation. He told me that John had a condition called esophageal varices; varicose veins in the esophagus, which had ruptured, producing the bleeding. One week ago I had been browsing through a medical dictionary. I just happened to see information on this condition and read the description of it. Dr. Cornell looked genuinely surprised when I told him I knew what that was. He began to describe to me his plan of treatment, which would involve placing a breathing tube down John's throat, re-inserting the endoscope and placing tiny rubber bands onto the varicose veins which would choke them off.

The veins would, in time, shrivel up and break off the esophageal wall, passing through his system without even being noticed. Isn't technology wonderful? And so amazing is the human body. I smiled and thanked Dr. Cornell, sending him on his way to work his magic. It would be better if he didn't realize that I knew John almost died a few minutes ago. We could discuss that later.

Dr. Cornell's magic worked wonders. He successfully banded 8 varicose veins that day, and John would be ready to go home in 2 more days. We had no idea what could have possibly caused this condition. We never connected it with his enlarged liver, spleen and slightly elevated liver function. We would learn about that much later. The resident doctor who discharged John suggested he be evaluated for liver transplant. John didn't pay much attention to what the resident doctor was saying. He leaves the details to me. I can remember thinking 'he will never agree to that.' I let it go, and never mentioned it to John.

Ok . . . So THAT Was Scary!

We followed up with Dr. Cornell, who turned out to be a delightful man who spoke calmly and distinctly. His plan was to follow up and repeat the endoscope procedure at 6 month intervals, banding any new veins if there were any growing. He told us he suspected that John had the beginning of cirrhosis. I learned that one can live for years with cirrhosis before any symptoms begin to develop and that the liver can actually function on reserve for a long time. Maybe we would just learn to live with this. John never drank, smoked or did anything else that would intentionally harm his body. He would probably die of old age before his liver gave out. His biggest problem is worrying about things that don't matter and not getting enough sleep, thus producing heart problems, but those had already been fixed when he had the heart surgery. I told Dr. Cornell that I had seen what happened at the hospital when John had stopped breathing. He did acknowledge that John had, in fact stopped breathing. We were very grateful to him for having saved John's life.

January, 2008—Dr. Cornell banded 3 more very small veins in John's esophagus. We were scared and worried the night before the procedure after what had happened last July. John had stayed up late the previous night typing on his computer. The next morning the procedure went well and we were home by that afternoon. We took a nap. When I put my hand under my pillow I found an envelope with a typed page in it. It was the page that John had been typing last night. There were instructions on it. It began with him saying that if I was reading this, something had gone horribly wrong during the procedure, followed by instructions for his funeral arrangements and an apology for leaving me with two sons still at home, not yet out of their 20's. I cried at the thought that this could have become a reality.

But all was good now. I could file that letter for future reference, hoping I would never have to use it. We could go back to normal and get on with our busy lives. And that's what we did.

John was not able to have another endoscope in July of 2008 as originally planned. He had his top teeth extracted and was fitted for a top denture. With so much going on inside his mouth we felt it would not be a good idea to have a procedure done which would involve putting anything down his throat or irritating his mouth.

Long Journey . . . First Step

January 26, 2009: The nightmare begins! Dr. Cornell checked John for more bleeding varices. The good news was that he had found none, but something was bothering Dr. Cornell. He wanted to know why John's liver and spleen were enlarged, more so than on previous studies. He wanted John to have an ultrasound of the area so that he could get a better look. We thought 'ok. We'll get back to you on that.' and figured we would deal with it when ready. That was not to be. Dr. Cornell was way too efficient for that. The next day we received a phone call from his office with instructions of where and when to report for an abdominal ultrasound.

And so we went. The ultrasound was followed by an MRI that showed the grey area that Dr. Cornell wanted a better look at. This would be the second time he saved John's life. The MRI showed 3 lesions in the right lobe of John's liver, the largest being up into the dome of the liver. He would need a biopsy.

February 4, 2009: John had his biopsy done. It was a relatively easy procedure and all went well. The hardest part about having a biopsy is waiting for the results, which would take about a week.

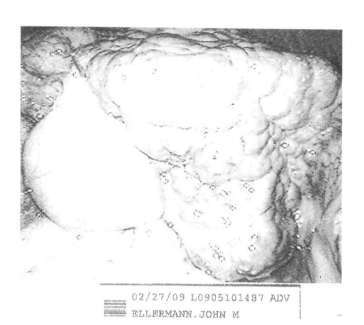

02/27/09 L0905101487 ADV
ELLERMANN,JOHN M

A Most Unusual Day

February 11, 2009: The sun was shining and it was an unusually warm day. The temperature would soar into the 60's that day which was unusual for the middle of February in Northeastern Pennsylvania. But nothing about this day would turn out to be 'usual'.

We were up bright and early for our 8AM appointment with Dr. Stephen Volk, a local hematologist/oncologist, another delightful man who would become part of a growing list of doctors we would see. Dr. Volk informed us that the biopsy results were inconclusive, which was probably good news. John had also had a tumor marker test which resulted in a normal to low result, another good indication that there was nothing to worry about. Just to be sure, the biopsy was sent to another lab to double check the inconclusive results. Dr. Volk assured us that if anything was wrong we would hear from him promptly. We drove home excitedly, stopped at our church, and told Pastor Doug the good news. The weather was so beautiful that I wanted to take a long drive. I decided to drive to New Jersey and visit John's Aunt Ruth so I could explain the whole story to her. It's much too difficult to explain all this over the phone, especially if the person you are explaining it to has limited medical knowledge and trouble with their hearing. All would be joyful in our little world now, or so I thought.

I arrived near where Aunt Ruth lived and stopped at a local diner for some take out food. Aunt Ruth and I would have lunch together and I would tell her all about our good news. I called John to tell him I had arrived safely. He told me he had just gotten off the phone with Dr. Volk. It seems the second biopsy report had shown that John had Hepatocellular Carcinoma, a slow growing cancer confined to the liver. This was like a cruel joke compared to the good news we had received this very morning. I felt like I wanted to drop the food right there, run to the car and drive home, but Aunt Ruth was expecting me. What would I tell her now? And what of John, alone and frightened upon hearing this latest news?

I walked into Aunt Ruth's kitchen trying not to look as if I was about to cry. I quickly served her the food and took a few bites for myself. I was too nauseated to eat, and told her the news I had just heard. Aunt Ruth prayed with me and sent me on my way.

I couldn't wait to get back home to John. I cried all the way home and tried to imagine how our lives would be from now on. I secretly wished I would get into an accident with a tractor trailer and God would mercifully spare me of what lied ahead. But what of the poor tractor trailer driver who would run into me? Our son, Jimmy is a tractor trailer driver. He risks his life every day when he gets behind the wheel in hopes that someone doesn't pull out in front of him or make some other erratic move that may cause an accident. Maybe that poor tractor trailer driver would be blamed and lose his license and livelihood. Possibly, even his freedom. I couldn't do that to another person. Most of all, what of John? Who would take care of him in my absence?

I pulled into the driveway, ran quickly into the house and hugged John like I would never let him go. He asked me "What about Pastor Doug? We'll have to tell him the bad news." I drove over to church and met with Pastor Doug and his wife, Karen. I told him I was all alone in the world now and would have to be strong for John, myself and our sons. How would I expect them to share this burden with me? Pastor Doug assured me that I was not alone. I would need to make John and the rest of my family a part of this perilous journey that we would walk through together. John especially needed to know that we were shoulder to shoulder, facing the unknown. Pastor Doug offered to come to our house and counsel us as often as needed, beginning with tonight, and told us he would see us later.

I left Pastor Doug's office dazed and confused. I called my best friend, Yvonne. Yvonne and I had become friends years ago when our sons were in kindergarten together. What started as a casual acquaintance would grow deeper over the years. Yvonne had explained the Gospel to me and shared with me the Good News that Jesus went to the cross for my sins.

Up until that time I had believed that God was "up there" and we were "down here" and if we behaved ourselves we might get to spend eternity with Him. It was never personal until Yvonne explained it to me on that beautiful Spring morning at the Franklin School playground. My reply was

"It sounds too good to be true. I want to know more." And learn more I did! She taught me as we enjoyed fellowship together over the next handful of years. When we moved to PA I heard her very words echoed from the pulpit of Trinity Wesleyan Church. Friendships often come and go, but my friendship with Yvonne became intense to the point of now being forever sisters in Christ. We are truly family.

I told Yvonne how frightened I was and how I felt all alone. She too told me that I was not alone, that He was with me every step of the way. "This is not the Jackie I know" she said, "Where is your faith?" I felt like I must have left it bundled up in the bed sheets somewhere when John had his biopsy a week earlier. Perhaps it had gotten tossed in with the soiled linens and swallowed up in some industrial strength laundering apparatus. Perhaps I would never again recover it.

After our session at home with Pastor Doug I sat on the couch beside John. I put my arm around him and asked him if he was scared. He buried his head in my shoulder, shook his head yes, and cried. I held him and tried to comfort him as best I could, then helped him into bed. I quietly tip toed off to my laptop computer where I could look up some much needed information and get to know our "new enemy."

The Enemy

What I learned of John's illness was very scary. The harsh words jumped out at me from the website, cutting through me like a knife. "Liver cancer is a bad cancer. 95% of people who get liver cancer live about 3 to 5 months from the time of their diagnosis." That's it? Is THAT how much time we would have together? 3 to 5 months? By the following morning I could not even speak in a complete sentence.

In the morning I went to see Dr. Snyder, our family doctor. Dr. Snyder is a bright, enthusiastic woman who is very efficient about keeping records and reports from all of the specialists John sees. Picture her as the center of a web of medical reports piling in from all different sources to be properly sorted and filed where they can be accessed when needed. She had a copy of John's biopsy report and explained to me that the cancer cells were in clusters rather than strands, which was a good thing. The cells were definitely confined to the liver which was also good, meaning the cancer hadn't come from somewhere else and spread to the liver, which was usually the case with liver cancer. In her words, "If you're gonna have cancer, this is a good cancer to have if there is such a thing as a good cancer." She made a copy of the biopsy report for me to take home and gave me a prescription for Zoloft, a mild anti-depressant, so I could think and make decisions calmly. I left her office feeling a little bit better.

Treatment

The following week we went to see a cancer surgeon. Dr. Quiros was a gentle and caring man who was amazed that John's liver cancer had been discovered so early. He told us that they don't usually find liver cancer until it's too late. John had no symptoms, and Dr. Quiros was very hopeful that the cancer could be treated. His first option, since the cancer was confined to the right lobe was to remove the right lobe of John's liver, leaving him with the other half to regenerate. The liver is an amazing part of the body. You can't live without one, but if half of it is removed it will re-grow to 95% of its normal capacity in about 6 weeks. Truly astounding! The Bible says "I praise you because I am fearfully and wonderfully made; your works are wonderful, I know that full well." (Psalm 139:14) That is something to think about. Imagine losing half of your liver and having it re-grow to almost it's normal size in just 6 weeks!

I reminded Dr. Quiros that John had the beginnings of cirrhosis. That, he said, would rule out removing half of his liver, but there was another option. It's called Radio Frequency Ablation. He brought in a tool which looked like a child's toy. It had a 3 pronged probe on the end of a metal rod. It works by emitting microwave probes to the tumor and surrounding area, thus "frying the tumor until it becomes a crispy critter" and can no longer reproduce cells.

Well, this was simple! Where do we sign up to have this marvelous thing done? We scheduled an appointment for the surgery and went on our "merry way."

February 27, 2009: Radio Frequency Ablation day had arrived. Yvonne drove to our house the night before and spent the night so she could be by my side while I waited for what we all hoped would be a good outcome following John's procedure. The three of us arrived at the hospital very early so John could be checked in and prepared for what would be a two hour operation. Pastor Doug came, prayed with us, and left once John was whisked away to the surgical area.

Yvonne and I settled in and made ourselves comfortable in the busy waiting area. I watched as family after family members received good or bad news, silently rejoicing or sympathizing, depending upon their loved one's outcome. It would be a long two hours.

Not as long as we had anticipated. Dr. Quiros appeared in the doorway 45 minutes later and motioned for me to follow him to a small private conference area. He showed me an 8 1/2 x 11 glossy photo that he took of John's liver using a laparoscopic camera. I had never seen a liver before and had no idea what I was looking at. This was definitely not for the faint of heart! Dr. Quiros explained to me that a normal liver is oblong shaped with a dome toward the top right. It is dark brown and has a smooth texture, resembling a mahogany table or desk top. "Much like this" he gestured to a piece of furniture in the room.

John's liver looked nothing like that. It actually resembled an old, grey sponge like the kind they use to wash cars with; lumpy and bumpy and full of craters and jagged edges. Dr. Quiros told me that John's cirrhosis was much worse than anticipated. "As a matter of fact," he told me, "if someone were to show me his blood work and this picture together I would think I was looking at results from two different patients." He went on to explain to me that he would not be able to perform the radio frequency ablation procedure without doing significant harm to John's surrounding liver. There was a possibility that John could bleed to death. The liver is a very vascular organ. Dr. Quiros was not about to take that chance but there were other options. He would return to the operating room, get John into recovery and then meet with us to discuss those options.

I returned to the waiting area ashen faced and tried to quietly and calmly explain to Yvonne all that I had just been told. I felt like every eye in the waiting room was on me to see if I would smile or cry. It seems that when I am in a crisis I want to find a hiding place in some obscure corner and be alone with my panic.

The old adage, 'never let them see you cry' seems to ring true with me. I'm not supposed to panic—just be strong for other people when they do.

Shortly thereafter we were directed to the recovery area. I was relieved to get out of the waiting room with all the eyes upon me and be able to hide behind a curtain in the small room where John slept.

John woke up a short time later and asked me if they were able to ablate the tumors. I told him "No, but there is another treatment." He then asked me, "Am I gonna die?" to which I answered "No." By this time, Yvonne could no longer stay in the room without showing her feelings. She had lost both of her parents to cancer and the scene playing out before her brought back painful memories. She retreated to an area across the hall, hid behind a curtain and cried. One of the nurses thought perhaps she was John's wife and was too distraught to handle the bad news, leaving another relative to tend to John.

John asked me again. "Please. Tell me the truth. Am I gonna die?" Again I answered no, but I knew he was thinking of what had happened when his mother was diagnosed with cancer. The doctors had told us there was nothing they could do and ten days later she was gone.

Dr. Quiros entered the room as promised, and I was glad to see him. I explained to him what had happened with John's mother and how similar this situation seemed to him. Dr. Quiros assured us that John was not in a hopeless situation and would not die. There were other ways to choke off the blood supply to the tumor, and in the coming weeks he would explain them all to us, finding the one that would work best for John. Ultimately, the most ideal option would be a liver transplant.

By this time, Yvonne had consoled herself enough to join us and hear the details that I was unable to comprehend in my present state of mind. I had been bombarded with so much medical information in the past hour that my brain felt as if it was about to explode. Yvonne told me later that she distinctly remembered Dr. Quiros telling us that "It's not the cancer that's the problem. It's the cirrhosis, which is a progressive disease." Progressive. I hung onto that word. Progressive. Not terminal. People lived a long time with cirrhosis and didn't even realize that they'd had it. I asked Dr. Quiros if John could get a liver transplant. "I don't know." He answered. "Maybe, but the waiting list is quite long, you know." 'It will be even longer if we don't get him on the list right away' I thought out loud.

Dr. Quiros went to work quickly, hurrying off to his office to have his staff contact a transplant center, thus getting the necessary paperwork started. In the meantime, John would have a revolutionary treatment aimed at choking off the blood supply to his tumors. We had a plan.

The Plan

March 17, 2009: John checked into St. Luke's Hospital for his revolutionary new treatment. It's called SIRSpheres. (Selected Internal Radiation) First they perform an imaging test which they call "mapping". In this way, they are able to determine where the blood supply is that is feeding the tumor. One week later we would come back and John would be injected with tiny glass beads that were filled with radiation. These little radioactive beads are about 1/3 of the width of a human hair but they are formidable weapons against a cancerous tumor. They are flown in from Australia where they are manufactured and must be inserted into the body within two hours of arrival at their destination.

The beads were injected into the blood supply of John's tumor, where they would choke off nourishment to the tumor and render it inactive. Then over a 3 month period, the beads would break open and emit radiation to the tumor in attempt to shrink and destroy it. Whoever thought of this was truly a genius! We were told specifically to not have any imaging studies done until 3 months after the insertion of the beads. The tumor swells before it shrinks, thus making the tumor look much larger than it actually is. Dr. Quiros didn't want a transplant team looking at an enlarged tumor and coming to a conclusion that it would be too aggressive to consider a liver transplant. Meanwhile he worked diligently with his staff to find a transplant center who would evaluate John.

The wheels of medical science turned quickly. We were contacted by phone and received a follow up letter with instructions for when and where to report for an evaluation. We did all we could to allow this process to run smoothly and efficiently. We went to the medical records department in the hospital where John had been treated with the SIRSpheres. We needed to retrieve the imaging discs and data that went along with that treatment. We wanted the transplant doctors to have all they needed at their fingertips.

St. Luke's is a wonderful hospital. All who work or volunteer there are always ready and willing to be of help to the patients and visitors. Someone asked us if we needed help finding the medical records department and offered to take us there using the shortcut. We stood waiting for an elevator which was near the morgue. The doors to the outside of the building opened and two technicians appeared wheeling a gurney with a body bag on it. John and I both looked at each other and, at the same time, thought the same thing: 'I wonder what that guy's liver looks like'.

House, MD

April 20, 2009: Evaluation day had arrived. We had received a letter with specific instructions about what would take place on this day. There is much we would learn. We were to arrive at the hospital's transplant services department promptly at 7:30AM. We were instructed to bring all of John's insurance information with us, along with the release forms we had filled out so that they could obtain John's medical records. We were also told to bring lunch or make arrangements to eat, as this would be an all day affair. John was not to eat or drink anything after midnight the night before. There would be numerous blood tests. John is diabetic, and since he could have nothing to eat I wasn't able to give him any of his insulin that morning.

Our sons, John and Jimmy had come along with us in anticipation of learning all they could about being a living donor. Being identical twins, they felt John had 2 good chances of receiving half of a good liver from one or the other. Jimmy and his friend, Joe, who he worked with, had seen a newspaper article about a man from our area who underwent a liver transplant recently. I was amazed to learn that age and time on the waiting list are not the deciding factors that will determine how soon one gets a liver. When we first started talking about the possibility of transplant I said to Jimmy, "If they have a 26 year old man and Dad, who is 64 years old who are they gonna pick? Probably the 26 year old because he's got a longer projected lifespan." Jimmy told me that he had read that's not how it works, and he was right!

```
                                              4-20-09
Dad

I WANT YOU TO KNOW HOW MUCH I
LOVE YOU. WERE GOING TO PULL THROUGH
THIS. THE NEWS HAS BEEN HARD ON
ME AND ITS COST ME ALOT OF SLEEPLESS
NIGHTS. WERE GOING TO FIGHT THIS
AND YOU JUST HAVE TO REMAIN POSITIVE.
IM GOING TO TELL THEM AT WORK THAT
I MAY NEED SOME MORE DAYS OFF OF
WORK FOR THIS ALL THE TIMES YOU
HAVE HELPED ME IN MY LIFE WITH WORK
AND FIRE CO. ITS NOW MY TURN. WHAT
EVER YOU NEED WETHER ITS FISHING,
POST OFF. GOING TO THE STORE, EVEN SPENDING
TIME AS FATHER AND SON. AND MOST IMPORTANT
MY LIVER. THATS RIGHT ITS READY FOR YOU
WHEN YOU NEED IT. I WOULD THROW EVERYTHING
AWAY. FRIENDS, FIRE CO, MY TRUCK, AND WORK
JUST TO KEEP YOU. DONT GIVE UP! IM HERE
AND WILL ALWAYS BE. I LOVE YOU TO MUCH
TO LET YOU GO!

                        LOVE YOUR
                          SON,
```

The transplant center was in the heart of a large metropolitan area. We made arrangements to stay at a nearby hotel the night before so that we could arrive early and be on time for our all day appointment the next morning. We arrived promptly at 7:15AM and found our way to the transplant services department. To our surprise, the door was locked and there were no lights on inside. I had the letter with me and double checked the date and time. We were here on the right day, and the right time too.

I looked around, bewildered, at the hallway, which was built of marble and had very high ceilings. Every sound echoed from the cold stone walls and ceilings. In the middle of the hallway was an oblong cement slab where people were sitting. There were no other seats available. The walking wounded milled about the hallway or just leaned against the walls, staring blankly into the vast space surrounding them. There were no reading materials, no lights, and no windows. But there were nearly 35 or 40 people scattered about that hallway. Someone apparently noticed our bewilderment and asked us, "Are you here for liver transplant?" to which I replied "Yes". "You're in the right place" he assured us, so we leaned against the wall and tried to "blend in" with the rest of the crowd.

Sure enough, we were in the right place. At 7:30AM sharp an official looking person approached the door, swiped a card into the lock, opened the door, went inside and settled in behind a services window. When he turned on the lights, the people flocked to the door as if it were black Friday at Wal-Mart. John and I, Jimmy and John looked on in dismay as the official told the crowd to form a line and take a number. Our son, John said to me, "It's like a deli counter. You give them your number and they give you a liver in a bag, then you take it down the hall and they put it in." "We'd better get on line before they run out of livers!" I exclaimed. "I'll take a plain one without onions. I'm not fussy!"

We didn't have to take a number. We were herded into a small room with a dozen or so other people to watch a 45 minute presentation given by the liver transplant coordinator. The purpose of the presentation was to explain the evaluation process and what happens once you are placed on the waiting list. There is much we would learn that day, and it turned out that this would be the most productive part of the whole trip. The transplant coordinator proceeded to explain the waiting list process. Placement on the waiting list is determined by the MELD score, which stands for Model for End stage Liver Disease. The MELD score begins with a total of 6 points and ends with 40 points; 6 being the least sick and 40 with weeks or perhaps hours to live.

"Some of you are here because you have liver cancer" she explained, "which will give you an automatic score of 22 points." I made a mental note of that and did the math. John would get 22 points for liver cancer, and who knows how many extras for just having cirrhosis in his liver. "We will transplant your liver with a total of 28 points" she went on to explain. To me this was good news! With 22 points and a few extras, John would win the "liver lottery" and this bizarre contest would be over by next week.

The transplant coordinator showed some slides which contained statistics about the size of liver tumors and the criteria they use as guidelines for transplant. If a tumor is 3 centimeters or greater they consider it too aggressive and will not consider the person a candidate for transplant. In some cases, they consider the Milan criteria, which is named after transplants done in Milan, Italy. In those cases, a person may have a single tumor that is no bigger than 5 centimeters. John's tumor was slightly larger than 5 centimeters. We were hoping the SIRSpheres would shrink it down to below 5 in order to meet the Milan criteria.

She went on to explain that they have an excellent cancer center in their hospital. "We have radiation treatments, chemotherapy, chemo-embolization where they inject radiation directly into the tumor, but we don't do SIRSpheres. We have heard of it but we have no data on how well it works." I made a mental note of that too.

Next we met with the social worker. We spent all of 15 minutes with her while she reviewed John's insurance information to make sure he had adequate insurance to pay for a liver transplant and subsequent follow up treatment. Then we were directed to the nutritionist who spoke to us about food. During this time, John was whisked away to have blood taken for cross-match, which determines blood type and other things relevant to receiving a new liver. When he came back into the room the nutritionist was still there talking with me about types of foods that keep your liver functioning properly. "Oh. You're still talking about food." John said calmly. "It's making me hungry."

There had been no time for the lunch they reminded us about in their letter. By the time we would find our way to the cafeteria it would be time for another consultation with yet another specialist. First impressions are lasting, and we didn't want to give anyone the impression that we didn't care enough to show up on time for a consult. (Keep that in mind; 'first impressions are lasting'.)

By this time it was mid afternoon and there had been nothing to eat or drink for John since midnight the night before, as per their instructions. He told this to the nutritionist while I reminded her that he was diabetic. "Oh, my God!" she exclaimed in a panic. I guess she thought that John would pass out right there in front of her since he hadn't eaten in so long and had just given the technician 17 tubes of blood. Perhaps his blood sugar would "bottom out" and then they would have a real crisis on their hands!

A nurse was immediately dispatched to find some juice and graham crackers for John. Jimmy and John returned at the same time from the cafeteria with a slice of pizza which tasted like cardboard garnished with spaghetti sauce. To John and me it tasted like a gourmet meal.

As John enjoyed his cardboard feast we were introduced to various members of the transplant team, which included the surgeons. One of them asked John if he had ever taken oral chemo drugs, like Nexavar or Sorafineb. He never did, and they told us that was a good thing because if he had, it would have ruled him out as a candidate for transplant. That was another important fact I learned that day.

Now we were ready for the grand finale. If you have ever watched House, MD, you will fully understand this next encounter. In case you are not familiar with Dr. House I will explain briefly. House, MD is a television series about a small group of doctors who are learning to practice medicine from the very knowledgeable and equally rude Dr. House. He is a walking, talking medical encyclopedia with absolutely no bedside manner.

That's the interesting thing about the show. The more rude he is to the patients, the more bizarre and intriguing the story is. We had watched it several times. In each story the patient had liver cancer. We learned a lot about liver cancer from watching Dr. House.

The head of transplant services entered the room with John's chart in hand. We both looked on anxiously while he reviewed the information, flipping pages and frowning at the data on the clipboard. Without looking up, he exclaimed in an annoyed tone, "Your tumor is too big. Why did they send you here?" We were stunned at his "House-like" demeanor. Fortunately, God has blessed me with being a quick thinker in times of crisis. I had in my possession the glossy photo of John's diseased liver, which I had planned to use as my "reason" in case we were met with resistance, which we were experiencing now. I gently pushed the picture under his nose and gave him a minute to look at it in hopes that it would soften his demeanor. "That's why we're here." I explained, to which he replied, "That is a diseased liver." 'Well, duh!' I thought. I didn't like this guy from the get-go and I was becoming more and more angry by the minute. Poor John just sat there in shock. The doctor told us John had to have some treatment to shrink the tumor to which I replied, "He had SIRSpheres." The doctor cut me off in mid sentence, telling me that SIRSpheres work only 20% of the time. I looked across the room and saw that John was looking more and more discouraged. Now I was ready for a fight! "Let me ask you something, Dr. House." I exclaimed. (John couldn't believe I actually called him Dr. House! I think the doctor was flattered.) I went on to explain that we had heard from the coordinator earlier in the day that they don't do SIRSpheres at that facility and had no data to back up how well they work. "How do you come up with that figure?" I asked him. He answered, "Well, you'll have

to have an MRI or something to see if the tumor shrunk."
I remembered Dr. Quiros' warning: "Do not have an MRI
until 3 months have passed." We didn't want them to see
a swollen tumor that would appear larger than it actually
was. All I could think at that point was 'we need to get out
of here!' I told Dr. House we would get back to him, took
back my glossy photo and left. On the way home John told
me he didn't care if he died. We would never set foot in that
place again.

We drove home amid rush hour traffic and uncomfortable
silence, neither John nor I wanting to verbally express what
was on our minds. Once home, we crawled into bed and I
held tightly to John. I listened while he quietly sobbed until
he fell asleep. I placed my hand over where his liver was and
silently prayed, "God. Please take this disease away and let
him live." In my quiet moments alone with God while John
slept, many times I found myself near speechless and could
only pray that simple one word prayer: "Live."

Hershey

A few weeks later John had another scan done to determine how well the SIRSpheres were working. True to their promise, the little beads were busy. The blood supply had been choked off and the tumor was in-active but had still not shrunk. Dr. Volk had given us this good news and we also went to see Dr. Quiros. We told him about our less than pleasant experience at the transplant center. He was deeply troubled by this and recommended another center. We also went to see Dr. Cornell who told us that he had experienced some communication problems with the center we had attended. He also thought another center would be a good idea.

Hershey Medical Center was highly recommended. Every person in the medical field who we spoke to had good things to say about Hershey. Arrangements were made for John to be evaluated there. We were off to a flying start again.

We received a letter from Hershey Medical Center explaining the evaluation process. It was very similar to the letter we had received from the previous transplant center. The instructions were the same: First appointment being at 7:30AM sharp. 'Please arrive early and have all the necessary forms filled out.' By this time we knew the drill. I had even contacted the previous transplant center with a request to forward all the information from our evaluation with them to Hershey. You can imagine what we were thinking: 'Here we go again. Same routine.'

July 20, 2009: Hershey turned out to be nothing like the previous experience. We were met in the hallway by kind folks who escorted us to where we needed to be. The first person we met was Allison, the transplant co-coordinator. She was an attractive young lady with curly blonde hair, blue eyes and beautiful white teeth. Her smile and pleasant demeanor made us feel relaxed and confident.

Allison explained some of the evaluation process to us and was encouraged to hear of all we had learned at the other center. That made her job even easier because she didn't have to explain certain things to us that we already knew. She gave John a script and escorted us to the lab where they drew about 17 tubes of blood. Then we had something to eat so that John would not be hungry or weak.

Next we met with the social worker. Her name was Velma, a very pleasant woman who was easy to talk to. She spent close to an hour with just John and I as we talked about many things. She was interested to hear about our life together, our family, and even our two cats. She really seemed to care about us, and this would be the first of many times we would talk with her.

Allison came to collect us again and took us upstairs to the 3rd floor where the surgery clinic was located. There we would meet Dr. Schreibman, the gastroenterologist. I could fill the pages of another book just describing Dr. Schreibman. He is the smartest person I have ever met, and a truly delightful and personable young man. We instantly liked him and told him how thrilled and relieved we were that he was nothing like "Dr. House" at the previous transplant center. He was very happy to hear that we had such confidence in him and he vowed to not be "House-like", doing all he could to help us. He then introduced us to the transplant surgeons and Dr. Kadry, the head of the transplant team. Dr. Kadry was also very pleasant, smart and confident that she could help us. We left Hershey that day feeling like once again we could see a light at the end of this long, dark tunnel.

Many people were delighted to hear of our good experience at Hershey. Our friends at church found renewed hope and encouragement to pray diligently, and pray they did! Every Wednesday morning a small group met and prayed, eagerly awaiting each new bit of news on our progress. There were many tests John would have to undergo before being placed on the waiting list for a liver. We felt renewed confidence that John would have a good outcome to all of these tests.

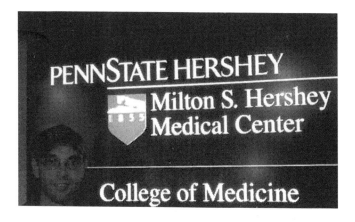

Testing, Waiting . . .
And Being Normal

The next few months were filled with testing and waiting, and more testing and waiting. Each time we saw Dr. Schreibman he would give us an update on the latest status of John's liver tumors. He would often say "I have good news and bad news." The good news was that the tumors had not progressed or showed any new growth. The bad news was that the biggest one at 4.9cm had not shrunk. I was beginning to feel anxious and couldn't understand why they couldn't just hurry up and get rid of that thing before it started growing again, becoming larger than 5cm.

Next came "the plan." The plan was to inject chemo directly into the tumors and wait to see if they would shrivel up and die off. This process is called chemo-embolization. They scheduled John for Oct. 14th to have this treatment.

Apparently John's liver was functioning quite well on reserve. We decided to take a trip to Denver, Colorado for a convention of a ladies group that I belonged to. John was quite active in the Knights Templar and had gotten me involved in their ladies group which is called the Social Order of Beauceant. Those ladies have groups who meet all over the country and once a year come together at a specific location for a five day convention of meetings, banquets and fellowship.

Our trip to Denver would be a nice diversion from all the medical poking and prodding John had to recently endure. Following the convention we would fly to Montana and spend five days with John's oldest son, Matthew and his family. It was a delightful and restful trip. Matthew was the perfect host and made us feel so at home. Matthew and I talked about John's condition and I explained all that I had learned.

John looked tired the first day in Montana but improved with a good night's sleep and enjoyed the rest of the trip. The only annoying problem was a small hernia developing in his right groin area. John wanted to be a good sport and tried a little bit of horseback riding anyway. So did I.

We flew home on October 1st, our 32nd anniversary. Jimmy and John were happy to see us. Our son, John came and picked us up at the airport. We had been gone 10 days and it felt good to be home even though we had enjoyed a good time in Colorado and Montana.

Life in PA was as busy as ever with much activity going on at the fire company. John attended the Tuesday night meeting with John and Jimmy and was happy to see his friends on the fire team. He came home earlier than John and Jimmy, which was usual for him. A short time later our son, John called me with a dilemma. It had been raining that evening and he had been standing alongside his pickup truck talking to a few of the firefighters. A small orange tabby cat had jumped into his truck and made a home for itself, curling up in the back seat. He couldn't just put the cat back outside in the pouring rain. What was he to do with the cat? I thought about it for a moment and then told him to bring the cat home. Being early October it wasn't very cold outside and our garage would make a sufficient shelter overnight. I found a large cardboard box and filled it with towels for the cat to sleep on. I placed a large plastic container at one end and filled it with cat litter. Then I placed 2 bowls inside the box and filled one with water and one with cat food. Once the cat was in the box I placed a screen over the top so it wouldn't jump out and have the run of "ground zero" in our garage. It would be so easy to get lost in there. John came out to the garage to see our "new guest" and announced, "We're not keeping it. Either he goes or I go." I smiled, waved and gently said "Bye." Then I assured him that I would make an effort to find the cat a home the next morning.

Morning came and I must say I didn't make much of an effort to find a home for the cat. I took the cat to the humane society where they scanned him to see if an owner's ID chip had been inserted. Three different scanners later they could find no chip. Needless to say, I was delighted. They asked me if I would like to leave him there and I answered no. Instead I brought him to the vet where he was examined and deemed a healthy and polite 10 month old boy. I brought him home, gave him a new place to sleep in our son, John's room and named him Redneck. To this day he is the life of the feline party at our house, chasing his two sisters, Taco Bell and Bug all through the house and entertaining us all with his antics. He has provided all of us with much joy and comfort during our darkest days.

October 13th, 2009 was a day that John had been looking forward to. The fire company had recently opened a sub station and planned an open house evening for the community to come and view the new facility. They expected a large crowd for the open house event. The firemen all looked so handsome in their new dress uniforms. John worked diligently directing traffic in the makeshift overflow parking lot in the grassy area across the street. This would be the last normal day of our lives. I would often remember that and would slow down to look as I passed that area on future trips.

Chemo

The next morning, October 14th we made the trip to Hershey where John would receive his first chemo-embolization treatment. The plan was for him to have two treatments spaced a month apart. He would stay overnight at the hospital and I would pick him up early the next morning. I stayed overnight at a nearby Holiday Inn but I stayed with John after the treatment as long as permitted. During this time he became extremely nauseous. In 32 years of marriage I had seen him throw up maybe twice. I knew this was a side effect of chemo but I kept telling myself this only happens to other people. It wouldn't happen to him because he had defied the odds with all of the treatments he had endured thus far. I tried not to look shocked and told myself he would be better tomorrow once I got him home.

Two nights later he woke up during the night and began gagging. I was very alarmed, as I thought this feeling would be gone by now. Things were beginning to get worse. The following morning I took him to our local emergency room where they did some blood work and took some pictures with a CAT scan. They diagnosed him with a back spasm which they felt came from having to lie still on his back for a few hours following the chemo procedure. They gave him a prescription for back pain. This didn't seem right to me. I didn't want to give him the pills because the warning label specifically read 'not for anyone with liver disease.'

The next few nights were progressively worse. John was in pain and having a hard time keeping food down. His appetite was becoming increasingly low and he was weak and tired. Our son, John woke up one night and heard the usual commotion and offered to take us to the emergency room. I told him I wanted to take Dad to Hershey because I felt it would be important for them to see him like this. They were planning another one of those chemo treatments and I wondered what a second one would do to him. Perhaps seeing him in this condition would produce a change in plans.

We are blessed with wonderful, caring sons. John cleared off the passenger seat and back seat of his pickup truck, warmed it up and drove us to Hershey at 3am. We were all so very tired when we arrived there. John was placed in one of the rooms in the emergency department. There was a small plastic chair for me to sit on alongside his bed. I squirmed and shifted and tried the best I could to make myself comfortable in the hopes that we wouldn't be there for too long. Our son had gone outside and napped in his truck. He slept better than I did and awoke to the sound of the medi-vac landing on the pad in front of him as daylight approached. At one point in sheer desperation I curled up on a blanket on the cold hard floor in the corner of the hospital room next to John's bed.

We were all glad to see Dr. Riley, Dr. Schreibman's associate arrive in the emergency department. He agreed that a second round of chemo would be out of the question for John and advised me to try and get as much nutrition into him as I could, using Boost or Ensure drinks to supplement his meals. I was angry and confused that this had happened. It seemed that the chemo treatment had destroyed John's reserve liver function and I expected the doctors to "fix this problem that they had created". Smiling and being polite I hid my frustration, asked questions and made written notes about what the next step would be. I knew in reality that these good doctors would never do anything intentional to harm John. Dr. Schreibman had warned us that there was a risk of side effects, and now here they were rearing their ugly heads. We left the emergency department later that morning. I was bound and determined to do all I could to keep John strong enough to survive so that he could get through this ordeal.

November 8, 2009: We continued to try to live life as normal as possible. I could see that John was becoming weaker as time wore on. Time, precious time was the hope we had to hang onto. That 'time' was slipping away from us as the effects of end stage liver disease began to take their toll on John's weakened body. The more difficult the battle became the more strength and knowledge God gave us to fight this new found enemy.

I read every booklet and pamphlet I could find on the subject of liver disease and corresponded with people online who either had the disease or were caregivers like myself. I had found this group by accident while one day surfing the web. The people at livercirrhosissupport@yahoo groups were the ones I had learned the most from. These are the heroes who are in the trenches either fighting this disease or advocating on behalf of someone they love. They are literally living through this nightmare. Through these good people I learned all about the transplant waiting list and much more useful information that would continue to prove valuable. God had, and continues to use these people in a wonderful way. In their darkest hours they reach out to help others who are just beginning on this perilous journey.

The Symptoms Begin

Since John was first diagnosed with liver disease the first thing I would do each morning was to look at his eyes and skin color. Every day the same thing: no signs of jaundice. All good. This particular morning as I helped John into the shower I noticed his belly looked swollen, much like I looked while pregnant with twins. This was not a good sign so I convinced him to let me take him to the emergency room. As scary as this was, it wasn't nearly as bad as the dreaded hepatic encephalopathy I had read about. The diseased liver is no longer able to effectively remove toxins from the body. The toxins get into the bloodstream and cross the blood/brain barrier, causing a person with cirrhosis to become disoriented and in severe cases, lapse into a coma. That sounded so scary! I helped John finish up with his shower and got him dressed comfortably in his sweat pants with an elastic waist, the only things that fit him these days. Off to the emergency room we went.

The good doctors at St. Luke's decided to admit John with a plan to tap the fluid which was accumulating in his belly, a condition called ascites. His ammonia level was slightly elevated so they would first consult with the doctors at Hershey and then start him on Lactulose, a syrupy liquid that removes toxins from the body, thus keeping the ammonia level down. John needed urgent attention. It all sounded like a good plan to me.

John was admitted to a room on the second floor; a private room with an added love seat that converted to a bed. I could room in with him. We were both happy about that. The nurse placed a bedside commode next to his hospital bed so that he could use it when the lactulose started to "work its magic." Nurses are some of the hardest working and under appreciated people in the medical field, and here were some of the best. Much of what they are required to do is physical labor, lifting patients, changing sheets, etc. They taught me how to do many things that John could no longer do by himself.

I enjoyed helping them, and John felt more confident too with me there by his side. I could think of no other place I would rather be. John asked to use the commode so I helped the nurse get him onto it. I sat in the room with him for a few minutes and then went out to the hallway to ask the nurse for some clean sheets. It would be nice for him to have clean sheets when he was placed back into the bed. When I came back into the room, John was still on the commode but slumped over sideways. I rushed to his side and slightly shook him, waking him up. He had fallen asleep. I had never seen anything like this before and it was a frightening sight. It was the first of many unusual side effects of liver disease that I would see.

Later that day a doctor came in to visit us and examine John. I gave him a quick update, explaining that we were in the process of getting John placed on the liver transplant list.

The doctor listened to my explanation and then asked us both if he could speak frankly. What could I say? I couldn't very well ask him to talk with me in the hallway out of John's earshot. John would be left there to wonder what we were talking about. The doctor had put me in a difficult position so the only thing left to do was to listen to what he had to say. He went on to tell us that we shouldn't get our hopes up of getting John a new liver. The list was quite long. I told him that I understood that, in fact there were currently 17,000 people on the list. That did not mean that John would become number 17,001. It would depend on how sick John was that would determine his score and placement. The doctor told me that was true but in his practice alone he had nineteen people on the waiting list. Now for those nineteen people maybe one liver would become available. Who would get it? Fortunately I had done my homework. I answered "The one with the highest score and the one that it matches. That liver will not match nineteen people, and who knows? John may be the one person it does match." He couldn't argue with the logic of that but he rattled off some grim statistics in an attempt to get us to face the stark reality of our present situation. I thanked him for taking the time to see us and ended the conversation.

We both lay quietly on our beds all night, neither one of us wanting to let the other know that we weren't really asleep. The next morning I went to John's bedside and told him I had been thinking about that conversation with the doctor all night. He confided to me that he had been doing exactly the same thing. "Here's the thing." I told him, "We believe in a God who doesn't care about statistics. He cares about people. He cares about you and me, and if He wants you to have a new liver you'll get one. He knows when and where, and even who it's coming from. Let's hang onto that hope." A day later John was released from the hospital. We had our instructions and new medicines to help manage his disease.

The Vision

Two nights later John woke up during the night in tears. I asked him what was wrong and he told me that he had experienced the most wonderful dream. He had dreamed that he became sicker and sicker and the Hand of God reached down and scooped him up. He found himself in the most beautiful place, standing before the Lord Himself. Surrounding the Throne of Grace were faces connected to white robes with no bodies; no arms or legs. I was amazed at this and asked him if he saw anyone he recognized. I thought perhaps a relative or an old friend he once knew. He told me that he had been instructed not to look around and not to speak. Jesus told him that he was in the house of eternity. He was preparing a place for him but he needed him to go back. His family and friends all needed him at this time and He was not ready for him yet. I asked him what Jesus looked like. He told me "Not like the pictures, but the voice, the voice was so gentle." He began to sob and told me he couldn't describe it. Then he told me, "I'm gonna beat this. I'm gonna make it." I knew he would.

More Plans

The next few weeks were filled with the activities of keeping appointments and undergoing hospital outpatient procedures. John would have fluid drained from his abdomen, and it would fill right back up again, much like a water balloon attached to a running spigot. This routine became our new 'normal' as John's appetite decreased and his belly expanded. I would be glad to see the doctors at Hershey again to hear of their next plan of treatment. Each time John had fluid removed he would feel a little better, but the better was only temporary. Even so, we were grateful for those good days.

We met with Dr. Cornell and I told him of our up-coming appointment with the transplant doctors at Hershey. We filled him in on all the details of the chemo-embolization and their plan for John to have another CT scan and MRI of his abdomen. This would determine how well the chemo worked at shrinking the tumors. I wanted to be ready for whatever the outcome would be. If it were negative, I wanted to make sure we had a "plan B" just in case their original one hadn't worked.

I had done some more homework on the internet and had read about a treatment called cyberknife. It's non-invasive, using a high dose of radiation beamed specifically at a tumor. I asked Dr. Cornell about it and he told us that he had in fact had a patient who was presently undergoing the treatment and would be evaluated for transplant. He gave us the name and phone number of the treatment center so that we could contact them if needed.

One week later we had an appointment at Hershey with Dr. Schreibman. He told us that he would do all he could to help us get John listed for a transplant but everything hinged on whether or not the chemo had worked and the tumor had, in fact, shrunk. I asked him if John could have the cyberknife treatment done.

I knew they didn't do that at Hershey but what if we went to the center where they did do it and then return to Hershey with the shrunken tumor? Could they transplant him then? Dr. Schreibman sadly shook his head 'no' and explained that it would be considered too much of a risk if the tumor did not respond to conventional chemo. I could not understand this and asked Dr. Schreibman "What's the difference if they shrink it one way or the other? A shrunken tumor is a shrunken tumor." Poor Dr. Schreibman was becoming frustrated with my desperation but tried his best to remain calm and compassionate. He explained to us that John was alive today because of all that they had done for him. I said nothing, but quietly thought, 'You injected him with chemo, took out whatever liver reserve he had left, and now somebody's got to clean up the mess!' I smiled through my negative thoughts and remembered that the doctors had no intention of doing John any harm. They were really doing all they could to help.

Dr. Schreibman went on to explain to John that there were other options. "What are they?" I asked. He told us about the oral chemo drugs like Nexavar and Sorafenib that would give John a good quality of life. He then told us that his dad had in fact, died of liver cancer. He had taken those oral chemo drugs, had a good quality of life and lived longer than anyone had expected. I thought 'Now I see. You're looking at John and seeing your dad, but this isn't your dad.' I didn't dare say this to Dr. Schreibman for several reasons; one being he was probably still grieving the loss of his dad and another being that I wanted to seem like we would be reasonable and listen to what these good doctors had to say. I quietly reasoned that Dr. Schreibman saw the glass half empty and I saw it half full. In sheer desperation I asked John to tell Dr. Schreibman about the profound vision he had on that night last month. John recounted his story about how he had been assured that God was not ready to call him home yet. Dr. Schreibman's reply was "Well, I'm not one to argue with the Man Upstairs,—or His Son." I would find a way to convince Dr. Schreibman that it was not yet time to give up. With God's direction we would find a way.

John would have the scans done on January 8th, 2010. We would try our best to celebrate Christmas and hope for good things in the New Year. Our brothers and sisters in the Lord continued to pray for us. They shared our hopes and dreams for the future and prayed diligently with me. We asked the Lord to give me the wisdom I needed to convince the doctors to do all that was needed for John.

The Letter

On January 1st that wisdom came. I sat down at my computer and began to type, writing a letter to Dr. Schreibman that came directly from my heart. I had been thinking long and hard about Dr. Schreibman. He is a young, energetic and attractive man; and so very smart. I envisioned him as perhaps the most popular boy in his graduating class at high school followed by being "the big man on campus" at college. Someone that popular would surely be involved in sports and lots of other extra curricular activities. I would use a "team analogy", explaining that we and the doctors were part of the same team. We were not the opponents, neither were they. The opponent was the disease. If we give up now it would be like forefitting the game and automatically letting the opponent win. We wanted to be good team players and we were in this game to win. We understood that there were risks involved but if no one ever took a risk, would there even be such a thing as a liver transplant? Suppose we took that risk and something went terribly wrong? I would still know that they had done everything humanly possible to save John and I would be eternally grateful for their efforts. I asked them, "Please don't give up on us. Where there is life there is hope." I would hand carry my letter tomorrow to Hershey when John had his scans.

Then the phone rang. It was the nurse from the radiology department at Hershey. She rattled off the usual instructions regarding fasting, medications and what time to report for the scan. Then she told me that the report would be sent to Dr. Kadry. "Dr. Kadry", I thought. She was the head of transplant. She was the one who needed to see this letter first. I quickly changed the greeting in my letter from Dr. Schreibman to Dr. Kadry and Transplant Team. I did nothing to change the contents. The next morning I told the receptionist at radiology that I had a very important letter for Dr. Kadry. She told me that Dr. Kadry was in the building that day and she would personally see to it that the letter was delivered. God was watching from above and He was hard at work! The plans we make! But nothing goes un-noticed under His watchful eye. Our job now was to carry on with life as usual and not give up hope.

The following is a copy of the letter:

January 1, 2010
Dr. Zakiyah Kadry and Transplant Team
Re: John M. Ellermann
Dr. Kadry and Team:

We were very encouraged to hear that the chemo—embolization did some good and the tumor has shrunk and is now inactive. That was good news and certainly brightened our holidays. We are hoping that the news from the next scheduled biopsy is good as well, and we are prepared as we continue to work together on the road to improved health.

While reflecting on all we have gone through thus far it brings to mind how we have all worked together as a team to produce a good outcome. When I think of a "team," I think of how we are trying to defeat our "opponent" which is cirrhosis and liver cancer. Since we are all on the same team John and I want to be valuable players and play to win.

There are some things I have observed, particularly since Oct. 14, 2009 when John had the chemo treatment. We arrived home the following morning to find both of our sons (who live at home with us) were sick at that time. One of them even had a fever. I was concerned that John would catch whatever they had, as his white blood count was low from the treatment. He had not yet had a flu shot. I am happy to say he "beat the odds" and didn't get sick. From this alone I get the impression that he is stronger than we think sometimes.

Despite the fact that his liver has been weakened by the chemo treatment, he seems to be doing quite well. In the past handful of weeks his appetite has improved and his energy level is also much improved. He is managing well as he keeps a regular schedule of medications and faithfully takes lactulose twice a day. He has a good attitude and a strong determination to do whatever it takes to make himself well again.

We understand the team's hesitation to proceed with transplant option due to the possible risks involved. Maybe another tumor would develop, but also, maybe not. We feel that since he has beat other odds, such as not getting sick with a compromised immune system and the tumor shrinking with only a 20% chance of doing so, to be cautious at this time seems to us like "waving the white flag of surrender" or "giving up and quitting the game." We understand that the team of doctors at Hershey are concerned about risks, but if we didn't take risks where would we be now? Where there is life, there is hope and we are willing to take risks because there is much potential for John to have good quality of life, we hope, for many good years to come.

We know you are doing all you can to help us, and we are very appreciative of it. It is a privilege to be on your team. If you step out in faith and make a decision to place him on the list and transplant his liver, naturally we will be very grateful. If you proceed with this plan and something were to go wrong during or after the surgery, I can honestly say that I would still be grateful knowing you have done all humanly possible to save John's life. Perhaps God had another plan. As a team, we have all come so far. Please take a chance and don't give up on us now. We are so grateful for your help. Please include our thoughts in your decision.

An Almost Normal Weekend

Feb. 5, 2010: John had looked forward to this weekend for a long time. Once a year he and his Knights Templar Division Commander pals spent a weekend along with the state officers reviewing the latest changes and improvements in the group's procedure and protocol. The wives came along and enjoyed fellowship and shopping on their own, along with a banquet for the entire gathering on Saturday night. It was a great way to relax with friends and enjoy the beautiful facility at the Masonic headquarters in Elizabethtown, PA. Since I knew my way around nearby Hershey so well, I always offered to be one of the drivers for the shopping trip to the Hershey Outlets.

John was tired as usual but we packed our bags and I made myself comfortable behind the wheel for the drive to Elizabethtown. It was early in the day. The weekend events didn't start until 7PM. I was a little annoyed because John wanted to get there early. That was typical of John. Always the first one to arrive and the last one to leave. I asked him why he wanted to be there so early and he told me he had volunteered to help with the check-in as he had always done the previous years. I couldn't understand why he did that, knowing that he wasn't feeling well. I asked him why and his answer was "Because I want to make nice." "Never mind making nice!" I scolded. "You know you're not up to all that and if I hear you complain or whine about not feeling good we're packing up and coming straight home!" I drove on, mumbling under my breath while John enjoyed the ride.

I was worried about this trip because the weather forecast had been calling for snow with a significant amount of accumulation. We arrived in Elizabethtown nice and early as John had planned. We found our room, unpacked, and John helped out at the registration desk while I went out to dinner with a few friends.

John was tired and was only able to help for about an hour, then went to rest in our room. I brought back a portion of food for him but he didn't eat much of it. I was getting used to the fact that his appetite was getting smaller. I didn't think much of that. He wanted to rest some more, so I visited with the ladies for a short time then settled into bed.

Saturday morning we awoke to the promised significant snowfall. There would be no shopping trip to Hershey as planned. I could barely find my little PT Cruiser buried under the snow, and the plows had already been through the middle of the parking lot, creating a wall of snow behind my little marshmallow of a car. We resigned ourselves to plans of quiet fun and fellowship while the men had their meeting. We all gathered in the dining hall for a delicious hot breakfast to start our day. I was delighted to see John fill his plate and enjoy his food. But my joy would be short lived.

The men went off to their meeting while I sat in the circle of women. We all introduced ourselves, but most of them already knew me and were quite familiar with our situation.

I am so blessed to have these friends. They all cared and were eager to hear of the latest developments in our progress to get John a new liver. Again, Pastor Doug was right. When you reach out, friends will be there to help and encourage you. You are never alone in a perilous journey.

My cell phone rang. It was John. He wanted me to come to our room. He had only been in the meeting for an hour when he felt sick and needed to excuse himself. He hurried to the room and threw up his entire breakfast. He was weak and I knew we needed to go home. I had been telling the ladies when they had asked how he was feeling, about the conversation we had when we left our house to come to this event. We all laughed at the fact that I had told John 'if you whine, we're going home.' 'Isn't that just like a man?' we all agreed. I knew the ladies would want to know if John was all right so I reported back to them with "He whined, so we're going home!" We all chuckled, and I knew they felt sorry for us, but sometimes it's good to have a little humor in a bad situation.

Word traveled quickly among the Sir Knights that we needed to go home. They saw the condition of my car in the parking lot. True to their titles, those Knights in shining armor worked diligently with their snow shovels and car brushes so that we would have a clear path to the road home. They wouldn't even let me pick up a snow brush to help. We thanked our good friends and headed home. We arrived safely and John was glad to be back in his own bed. I was too, and relieved. If we needed a doctor at an odd hour it would be better to call from home. Two days later we did.

The Dreaded Hepatic Encephalopathy

Feb. 8, 2010: I woke John with the usual routine of Lactulose and blood sugar testing. He was lethargic; not his usual self. I told him he needed to take his medicine and have something to eat so I could give him his morning insulin. He told me he would get up soon. I waited for a few minutes and shook him again. He rolled over, smiled at me and announced, "You're a pain in the a**." I couldn't believe he could say such a thing to me. I sat on the edge of the bed and tried hard not to cry. Then it dawned on me. The dreaded hepatic encephalopathy had arrived! I pulled myself together and called for an ambulance. I reminded John that I had read about this and that he needed to trust me. He needed to go to the hospital. He seemed perfectly willing to go along with whatever plan I had in mind for him.

The ambulance crew arrived promptly. I gave them a written list of John's medications and told them he had hepatic encephalopathy. "What's that?" the paramedic asked. I told him John had end stage liver disease and followed with the abbreviated version of all the horrific side effects of this hideous disease. The ambulance crew were stunned that I knew so much, but this was my life now. Nothing else mattered. My brain had become a sponge and all of my free time was spent soaking up knowledge in an effort to beat the enemy that was attacking my husband's body and mind. I knew his spirit was in there somewhere and it was not broken. We would fight this enemy to the death and his spirit would win in the end.

John was admitted overnight to St. Luke's. The nurses and doctors took excellent care of him and brought his ammonia down to an acceptable level. His lactulose dose would have to be increased to 3 times a day. I would have to keep track of how many bowel movements he had each day so that the doctors could determine how well the lactulose was working. John was moving slower but his bowels were moving faster. He was a real good sport when it came to the indignity of wearing Depends.

Once we were at home I kept busy doing laundry, changing sheets and helping John to stay clean, dry and fed. I now had a 160 pound baby to take care of. Our son, John had installed a hand held shower head in our bathroom. It turned out to be a Godsend. I was able to get John into the shower and have him sit on a shower seat while I rinsed him off with the hand held shower head. It was also handy for cleaning out the bedpan that he used during the night.

This was our new "normal". I didn't know what normal was anymore. There was little time to think about what had once been. In those precious moments between giving meds, trying to get some nutrition into John and cleaning up, I would close my eyes and escape in my mind to our one and a half story Cape Cod house in Union, NJ. Little John, Jimmy and I would ride our bikes around the neighborhood. I could still feel the wind in my hair while I sat and daydreamed of better times. We would visit with Yvonne. She lived around the corner from us. Little John and Bethie would spin around Yvonne's back yard in Bethie's Barbie car while Jimmy and Chris would busy themselves with other toys. Yvonne and I would solve the world's dilemmas over a cup of tea. Then we would say goodbye and ride to Dad's work only four blocks away where he would be just finishing up with his day's work. He would drive home slowly and we would ride alongside on our bikes to the house. Those were the happy times. Family, friends, and neighbors. Whenever something bad happened in my life I wished I had never left Union, NJ. It represented the happiest time in my life. I still get that same happy feeling whenever I pass through there to this day.

Now I had many other things to think about. I still had family. I still had friends, and most importantly, I had God. True to His promise, all through this struggle He had never left me. He directed my every move even though I wasn't always aware of it. I found new strength in the daily routine of taking care of John's every need, and I treasured each day that he was able to stay awake long enough to enjoy a TV show or just a few quiet moments together. This was how we were able to maintain a normal existence in the midst of chaos.

I tried hard to keep things normal for our sons, John and Jimmy. They went to work each day, came home and enjoyed a few hours of socializing with friends or responding to fire calls with the local fire company. Little John particularly made life seem normal. He has a way of bringing humor to situations. Being able to laugh made things so much more bearable. Jimmy also used humor to cope with the crisis that we were facing. One day while at work he took a magic marker and drew a dotted line on his abdomen where he imagined his liver would be. Inside the circle, he printed in bold letters: "In case of loss of life this organ is accounted for by John Ellermann, Sr." Hey, you never know. Suppose he were to have a fatal accident while on the road one day. He has designated "organ donor" on his driver's license. At least they would know what to do with the spare parts. We were doing exactly what Pastor Doug had suggested when this battle had first begun. We were leaning on and drawing strength from one another.

February 18, 2010: The dreaded encephalopathy returned! I woke John for his morning dose of lactulose and was once again reminded that I was a "pain in the a**." This time

I didn't take it so hard. It was my job to be a pain in the a** and I was getting very good at it. I calmly called for an ambulance. The same two paramedics arrived which meant I didn't have to explain the problem. They had already been given the end stage liver disease crash course. They asked John if he thought he needed to go to the hospital. He smiled and told them he was fine. Then they proceeded to tell me that they couldn't take him to the hospital against his will. Perhaps he would become resistant and hurt himself in the process of fighting them off. John would never do that. Even in his state of mental confusion he was not aggressive. He was more like a happy drunk, even though he never drank. I told the paramedics that he needed to be in the hospital. If his ammonia level continued to rise he would lapse into a coma and perhaps die. To my astonishment one of the paramedics responded by saying "Maybe he wants to let nature take its course." I knew John was not ready to die. I went to the kitchen, poured him a dose of lactulose and brought it back to the bedroom. I told them to "watch this" and I put the cup to his lips. He grimaced and turned his head. The paramedics looked at each other and then looked to the policeman who was with them. They asked for his opinion, to which he responded, "I'm a witness. He refused his medication so I would take him to the hospital." I was so grateful that the policeman was there. Now I knew that I had to obtain legal and healthcare power of attorney. We would make that our first priority once we dealt with this crisis. Two days later things were back to 'normal' again and we were able to get the power of attorney documents that we so desperately needed. Thank God John was able to make his wishes known to the lawyer and be of sound mind to sign the papers.

John's ability to concentrate on anything was becoming severely compromised. He was barely able to carry on a phone conversation with his friends from the Knights Templar. Those Masonic brothers called frequently and expressed their desire to help in whatever ways they could. Just hearing their voices on a daily basis was of great comfort to me.

March 2010

One day followed another and the next thing we knew it was the month of March. Winter was gone. Spring was becoming visible as the lawn was beginning to turn green. Flowers and trees began to bloom as little green buds poked up from the ground, straining their delicate stems toward the morning burst of sunshine. Little buds began to grow on the tree branches, a promise from God that all was becoming fresh and new again. Perhaps now was the time for something to bloom fresh and new in our lives as well. We had a new season of hope.

I had been elected President of my Assembly of Social Order Of Beauceant. John had encouraged me a few years ago to become active in this group, sharing my enthusiasm and pledging his support during my term as President. I had agreed somewhat reluctantly, and decided that if it made John happy I would get involved with this group. It turned out to be much like the Order of Eastern Star, which I had been active in during my younger days. At first I felt that I had gotten myself into something I just didn't have time for, but as I went to meetings and became more involved I really began to enjoy being a member of this group. John was not able to be my moral support as promised, but I now had a bunch of "sisters" who cared and stayed in touch regularly to keep my spirits up.

I had hoped that being President of this group for a year would be a pleasant diversion, and that is exactly what it became. My first meeting to preside over was to take place the second Wednesday in March. Now here's what happens on these evenings: The women have their meeting while their Sir Knights (husbands) enjoy each other's company with lively conversation as the wives are conducting their business. Then we all enjoy light refreshments before returning to our homes. There are only two Assemblies here in PA; one in Elizabethtown, and the other near Pittsburgh. Some of the members travel for a few hours to come to the monthly Assembly meetings. John and I have made many new friends as a result of these gatherings.

John was much too sick to travel with me to attend my first meeting. I was so sad and apprehensive, knowing he wouldn't be there, but I knew I had to fulfill my obligation to the group. I was relieved that Loie, Joan and Ant were planning to visit and would be here to watch over John while I was away for a few hours. Things turned out much different than I had planned, but by this time I was getting used to not planning anything.

I was happy to be having company. The last time Loie, Joan and Ant came was the weekend of my 60th birthday in November. John was just beginning at that time to feel the effects of end stage liver disease, but we still enjoyed ourselves and had a fun time. Loie and Joan are close in age to me. We have much in common. Ant had made me a birthday cake and Loie and Joan gave me a banner to wear that read "the big 6-0". I wore it for most of the day, even after we had gotten comfortable in our pajamas. They wanted to take pictures of me wearing the banner. "But I'm not wearing a bra." I exclaimed. "I'm n.b.!" (John had told me years ago that Loie and Joan had these "codes" when they were growing up that they used to speak to each other in. One of them was n.b. which meant "no bra.") They thought it was so funny that I knew about n.b. We laughed and laughed about all the crazy things we used to do. As the hours passed, we talked about when we were just kids while John and Ant looked on in amusement.

Family Visit

I was looking forward to another fun visit where we could laugh about what had once been and break up the daily routine of wondering what would happen next. What happened next was not the way I had hoped this visit would turn out, but I was still glad that Loie, Joan and Ant were here.

I woke John so that I could have him up and dressed before company came. He was very sleepy. Here we go again! Another round of hepatic encephalopathy! Today, of all days! I had hoped his sisters would see him doing a little better than expected. Perhaps in a few hours he would have his extra dose of lactulose and would be a little more alert. I decided not to panic and just do what needed to be done.

I quickly got dressed, made some cream of wheat for John, and called in a new prescription for his lactulose as the supply was running low. After a few morsels of food and his medicine he went back to sleep. I would wake him in a few hours to give him another dose. I fed the cats and sat down to read the paper. John had always loved to read the paper, especially the funnies, but he was no longer able to concentrate, even on the newspaper funnies.

Two hours later I gave him another dose of lactulose. The liver transplant coordinator had explained to me that when it seems like his ammonia level is higher than normal, I would be able to give him an extra dose. I would be the best one to determine John's ammonia level since I knew him better than anyone else. If he seemed lethargic or confused, that was an indication that his ammonia level was elevated. I understood the flexibility of this medicine because John is diabetic and also takes insulin. When his blood sugar is high I have to give him a little extra insulin. Obviously lactulose worked the same way.

John was sleeping peacefully when Loie, Joan and Ant arrived. I helped them bring their luggage into the house and told them that I needed to go to the pharmacy for John's medicine. John would be fine, sleeping while I was gone. Loie, Joan and Ant were anxious to see him but understood that he needed to rest. They agreed to listen for him if he woke up and called for me.

I arrived back home quickly, as I had learned to make all of my errands extremely short. Loie and Joan had settled in nicely, busying themselves by finding their way around my kitchen while Ant had made herself comfortable in an easy chair. The first thing I did was check on John. Loie and Joan followed me into the bedroom hoping to say hello to him. Loie told me that when she had gone in to use the bathroom she smelled something bad. Perhaps it was the cats' litter box.

It wasn't the litter box. I pulled back the covers on the bed. Oh, My God! The lactulose had worked and John had never even woke up and felt it. I rolled him over and told him we needed to get him into the shower to get him cleaned up. "I'm all right" he answered in a sleepy tone. He wasn't all right. I managed to get him to a standing position and told Loie to walk him into the bathroom. Joan began pulling the sheets off the bed but Loie stood there in shock. She was afraid to move him because she was afraid he would fall down. I showed her how to take hold of his forearms, walk backwards facing him and gently pull him along. Natural instinct would take care of the rest. Being pulled along, he would automatically walk. Ant, hearing the commotion, saw one quick glimpse of John and immediately ran to the kitchen sink where she threw up. Now I not only had John, but 3 more basket cases on my hands. How would I take care of John and calm Loie, Joan and Ant?

Between Loie and I, we were able to get John into the shower where I hosed him down with the hand held shower head. Joan had found some clean sheets and made up the bed. We tucked him back into the bed, and Joan went to check on Ant. She had settled down and somehow cleaned up her own mess.

The three of them were so upset they didn't know what to do next. We all sat down in the living room to calm ourselves. Loie and Joan cried and Joan asked me how I was able to manage this on a daily basis. I had never taken the time to think about it. For me this had all become routine. I explained lactulose to them and told them that I still needed to give him an extra dose. This may happen all over again but perhaps later on he would become more alert once the proper dose of lactulose had worked its magic.

It had already begun. By early evening, sure enough, John was much more alert. He was able to make his way to the living room to socialize with us. Loie, Joan and Ant were astonished at how much more alert he was, but that is the nature of this hideous disease. I was greatly relieved too that he was able to show them that he would be ok.

The "ok" was short lived. The extra lactulose had caused him to dehydrate. I called the ambulance again, and he was taken to the hospital. Once John was settled into a room I went out to dinner with Loie, Joan and Ant. I tried very hard to make life seem normal for them. They were good guests and knew they would have to entertain themselves while I tended to John at the hospital. I stayed with John for as long as I could.

In a way I was glad that John would be in the hospital while I was at my meeting with the Beauceant ladies. I knew that he would be well taken care of by caring and competent nurses and staff. His good friend, Dallas had come to visit with him during the day. Dallas belonged to the Knights Templar with John and the two had become very good friends recently. They often enjoyed conversation together. We had even invited Dallas to spend Christmas and Easter with our family, as he lived alone. We all enjoyed his company.

The Buzz Aldrin Affair

During this time while John was in the hospital, our good friends, Sandy and Les had stopped by for a visit. Sandy was my mentor in the Social Order Of Beauceant and Les had just finished his year as Grand Commander of Knights Templar of PA. We loved them so. Sandy was like a true sister to me. I had always wished I had a sister, and Sandy was one. They offered to take me out to dinner while Dallas visited with John. Dallas had brought along a Masonic magazine that he was excited about showing to John. There was a feature article in the magazine written by former astronaut Buzz Aldrin who also happens to be a mason.

My first meeting as President of Social Order Of Beauceant was indeed a pleasant diversion from the everyday life of end stage liver disease. The ladies all told me how much they enjoyed the evening and were anxious to hear about how things were going with John. They all encouraged me, wished me well and promised to help me in whatever ways they could. Just being with them was a help to me.

I arrived home from my meeting late; about 12:30AM to be exact. I thought about calling John but thought perhaps it would be too late. He might be sleeping. It took me awhile to fall asleep since I was wide awake from the drive home and all I had to think about. I finally dozed off around 1:30.

At 2:30AM my cell phone rang. It was John and he sounded anxious. He told me that he felt like he was on the verge of a psychotic breakdown. He was afraid that they would put him in the psych ward. 'Something must have happened' I thought, forcing myself out of my sleep. I told him to talk to the nurse about how he felt. I would call him back after he did that. I also told him that I would come and stay with him if he needed me to. I hung up the phone and waited for what seemed like the longest 5 minutes of my life.

Then I called the nurses' desk. The nurse told me that she had talked with John. He had seemed a little anxious at first but was much better now. She had even gotten a smile from him. I could come if I wanted to but she seemed to feel that he would be ok. I called John back and asked him if he had talked to the nurse. I wanted to see what he remembered. He told me that he had but he still felt very nervous. I asked him if he wanted me to come. He said he would feel better if I was there. I crawled out of bed and tip-toed out the front door being careful to not wake Loie, Joan and Ant.

The staff at St. Lukes are very caring and compassionate. They were happy to let me in after hours, escort me to John's room and find me a recliner to sleep in next to his bed. Thoughtful as they were, a hospital is not a place where one can fall asleep at the drop of a hat. I tossed and turned for a few hours and finally found a comfortable position in the recliner, drifting off to sleep.

I awoke to the feeling of a hand tapping my arm and John's voice telling me "Wake up! You're gonna miss it!" "Miss what?" I asked him, to which he replied, "the moon launch!" I looked at the TV, which was turned off and told him in a somewhat puzzled tone of voice, "There's nothing on TV. Is there supposed to be a moon launch?" "It's me!" He answered. "I'm Buzz Aldrin! I'm going to the moon!" I was so tired by this time, and in no mood for any 'hepatic encephalopathy' games, so I told him to "Buzz off and go back to sleep!" Obediently, he did.

A Bug

After another quiet hour I decided to go home and tend to my house guests. Loie, Joan and Ant had made themselves breakfast and cleaned up their breakfast dishes. They were excited about visiting John at the hospital. We would have a nice visit and then we would have dinner out. Joan was looking forward to a trip to the camping resort where our trailer was parked. She had only seen pictures of our trailer, and was anxious to see the real thing. I would entertain them for awhile, then go back to the hospital and spend the night with John. He seemed less anxious or confused when I was there with him.

When we arrived at the hospital we were informed that John had been moved to a private room to protect him from a virus that had been going around. The nurse at the desk had explained to me that it was a stomach flu. Even some of the nurses had caught it and they didn't want to take a chance with John in his weakened condition. We found our way to John's room. He was happy to see us.

John's plan of treatment was a series of swallowing tests. The doctors had suspected that something was wrong with John's epiglottis, the mechanism that permits swallowing. Supposedly, many sick and elderly people get this condition and must exist on thickened liquids. I had a gut feeling that hepatic encephalopathy was at the root of this latest complication but I wasn't about to argue with those in the medical profession. They obviously knew better than me.

My cell phone rang. It was the liver transplant coordinator. She told me that I needed to advise the transplant center at Hershey immediately whenever John was admitted to the local hospital. The transplant coordinator informed me that "he is pretty high up on our list." That was astonishing news to me.

The last I had heard, John was "status 7" which meant standby until another imaging study of the tumors could be done. The transplant coordinator wanted to know all the details of John's present condition. While she was saying that, Dr. Cornell walked in. Perfect timing! I handed him my cell phone and said, "It's for you." He went out to the hallway and had a detailed conversation with the liver transplant coordinator, then came back into the room and handed me the phone. He confirmed what she had told me about John being a priority on their list. I introduced Dr. Cornell to Loie and Joan. They were very pleased to meet the doctor who had saved their brother's life not once, but twice.

Dr. Cornell told us he planned to add a new medicine to John's growing list of meds. It's called xifaxin and it's used for traveler's diaharrea. He explained that it would help to draw the toxins out of John's intestines, preventing the contents of his intestines to turn to ammonia and cross the blood/brain barrier. Xifaxin is very expensive. Dr. Cornell was only too happy to write a letter to John's insurance company explaining that this medicine was medically necessary for this condition.

John's dinner arrived. It looked appetizing and I was enthusiastic about seeing how much I could get him to eat. It looked like too much for him to eat with his small appetite. I took his fork and did the 'one for me, one for you' routine in hopes that he would be encouraged to eat.

We said our "see you later's" to John and left to have dinner, followed by our trip to the campground. I then dropped Loie, Joan and Ant at the house and returned to the hospital to stay with John overnight. The nurses were happy to have me there with him. By this time I had learned to meet many of his physical and emotional needs. If something came up that I couldn't deal with by myself, the nurses would help me.

My cell phone rang. It was Yvonne. I went to a nice quiet area where we could talk. I was still wondering what the transplant coordinator meant by John being high up on their list and I was anxious to tell Yvonne all about it. The excitement of the day had left me with stomach pains and an irritable bowel. I was guessing this was all to be expected. I hung up with Yvonne and made my way back to John's room.

But something was not right. I felt extremely queasy. Maybe it wouldn't be a good idea to stay with John. I didn't want him to catch something if indeed I was coming down with the dreaded stomach flu. I remembered when his dinner had arrived and we shared it. The portion looked too big for him and made him lose his appetite. Now I was worried that my "cooties" had gotten onto the fork that we had shared earlier in the day.

I stopped by the nurses' station and told the nurse that I thought I had better spend the night at home. I was beginning to feel more queasy by the minute. I told her I would go into John's room to get my stuff that I had left there and I would say good night to him. I would be back early in the morning. She assured me that he would be well taken care of during the night.

I quickly grabbed my bag and said good night to John. When I walked out of the room—it happened! Everything I had eaten in the past few hours either came up or went down. I ran to a shower room that was close by in the hallway. The nurses heard the commotion and came running. Three of them stood there and asked me "Who's your nurse?" I couldn't even get an answer out between gags. The nurse from the desk came over and told them, "That's Mrs. Ellermann. She said she didn't feel good. We have to get her to the e.r.!"

By this time I had stopped throwing up long enough to tell them I couldn't go like this. I had a pair of pajama bottoms on that were a mess from all that had just poured out of me. The nurse grabbed a wheelchair and a pair of pajama bottoms and a diaper for me. She wheeled me to the nearest restroom. As if those poor nurses didn't have enough to do, now they had to take care of me. I felt so bad for them, and I was embarrassed besides.

I somehow managed to get cleaned up. One of the nurses took me to the e.r. The doctor there gave me some medicine and sent me home. I drove home and staggered into the house. Thank God I had a good supply of Depends. I went through 4 of them during the night. I don't know what I would have done without Ant. She took good care of me. She checked on me often and made me soup and toast. I called the nurses desk the following morning to check on John. So far he hadn't gotten the bug that was going around, but during the night three more nurses were sent home. They were dropping like flies all around him. Once again John had beaten the odds. I made a mental note to tell that to the transplant team.

A day later I was feeling better so I was able to return to John's bedside where I wanted to be. My houseguests had left for their return home. I missed them already. It's always good to have people nearby while you are going through a crisis. Their presence had been a real comfort to me and to John too.

John was released from the hospital a few days later with a plan for him to be on xifaxin along with lactulose and thickened liquids. A speech therapist would come to the house twice a week to work with him on strengthening his swallowing muscles. He enjoyed his therapy and diligently practiced his "gu" words every day to make his throat muscles stronger. Despite their instructions of thickened liquids he was able to swallow his pills whole with plain water. He often asked for water throughout the day. If he asked for it, I gave it to him. I felt that if his body craved water then he needed it.

Getting Weaker . . . And Sicker

I had brought my blender home from the trailer in the hopes of pureeing John's food. I bought vegetables, fruit and potatoes with renewed enthusiasm of getting a full meal into his belly. I also picked out some baby foods that I thought he might like. I could heat those up and make him a full meal accompanied by a Boost or Ensure shake. I was bound and determined to make him stronger, but it was not to be.

John spent much of his time in bed. He was too weak and uncomfortable to sit up in a chair for any length of time. Despite his time in bed the days went by quickly. We had a full schedule between the speech therapy, physical therapy and visiting nurses. The nurses came twice a week to check his vital signs and draw blood for his MELD score. (Model for End stage Liver Disease) Keeping track of this score was of the utmost importance to determine the urgency of John's need for a liver transplant.

We were, by this time, well equipped with all the necessary equipment to make our house into a makeshift hospital. We had a bedside commode, bedpan, mattress pads, Depends, and four hospital gowns to make changing and bathing easier. We also had a bedside tray much like the kind they use in hospitals. I used the tray often, several times a day as a matter of fact. I would place a basin on it, filled with warm water and shave John every morning, followed by a sponge bath. I knew that if I kept John looking good he would, in turn, feel good.

The bedside tray worked wonderful for mealtimes. One night I heated up baby food for John and placed the bowl on the tray. He seemed to be having more trouble swallowing that day so I felt it would be best for him to sit up on the side of the bed to eat. I helped him to a sitting position and sat alongside of him to help him with the meal. I placed a small amount of the food onto a spoon and put it to his mouth.

To my horror, his eyes rolled up and he passed out right into the bowl of food! I panicked! I had never seen anything like this before. I screamed, and our sons came running to see what had happened. Between the three of us, we cleaned John up and put him back to bed. The visiting nurse came and checked his vital signs which were by this time, stable. From that moment on I spent much of my time in the bed next to John. Each day I hoped for a better tomorrow.

Friends called, and when they did, John was unable to say much to them, much less concentrate on what they were saying to him. His mind was somewhat clear but he was so very tired.

The End Of March . . .
And Almost The End Of John

John had been the Knights Templar Division Commander of Division 9 for the past 3 years, a position he had enjoyed. He was the representative of the Grand Commander for his division of the state which consisted of our surrounding area. It was now time for him to turn over his duties to his successor, his good friend, Bob from Reading, PA. Bob called me and asked if he could stop by the house for a short visit with John, and collect some of the paperwork he would need to get started as the new Division Commander. This would be good for John to be able to visit with a friend, since he was no longer able to attend meetings. He missed his friends from Commandery, even though they called him often. Dallas and Frank had visited often, and we were grateful for that too.

I set up a time for Bob to come to the house. It was the morning of March 30th. I woke John with his usual routine of medicines, pureed food and morning grooming session. I then walked him to the living room and made him comfortable on the couch just in time for Bob's arrival. I had tried my best to prepare Bob for the visit. This was not John the way Bob had remembered him, and I was worried that Bob would be shocked at how much John had deteriorated physically.

Bob put up a good front. He greeted John, talked of the latest Commandery happenings and collected whatever paperwork he could find with my assistance. John was unable to carry on a conversation. He was too weak. All he could say was, "It's good to see you, Bob." Once Bob left, John wanted to go back to bed. It took all the strength I had to pull him up from the couch and get him back into bed.

March 31st was a day I will never forget as long as I live. John had his usual meds along with a few sips of water but something was wrong. I was hoping to get him through these next few days.

April 5th was our scheduled trip to Hershey where John would have the CT scan that would determine his placement on the transplant list. If only we could make it to that day! I could not get John to eat anything. Not so much as a morsel of food. Just a few sips of water. Dallas called and wanted to say hello to him but John kept falling asleep. I knew he was too weak to talk. I took the phone and went to the furthest corner of the house where John couldn't hear me. I told Dallas that John was dying.

I had seen and read about what I was experiencing today and I remembered when my mother-in-law died a few years earlier. We had called in hospice. The hospice volunteers had given us a book to read called "Crossing The Creek." It explained all the physical and emotional aspects of what happens when a person is dying. My mother-in-law was a textbook case, and now I was seeing the same thing with

John. Nothing had gone in or out of his system for almost 24 hours now, except for those few sips of water. In a desperate attempt to get lactulose into him I had filled a medicine dropper and put a few drops at a time onto his tongue. He was physically shutting down. Dallas came over, and I was glad he was there. I was so afraid of facing this alone. What would I tell John and Jimmy when they came home, and what would I tell the rest of the family? I needed help!

I sat and talked with Dallas while John slept; then Dallas went into the bedroom to see John. I called the transplant team at Hershey while Dallas sat with John. The transplant coordinator advised me to get John to St. Luke's. They would make arrangements to have him transported to Hershey as soon as he was stabilized. I went back into the bedroom to tell John of the latest plan. He weakly answered, "No hospital." I knew he was discouraged because he had been in the hospital so much lately and just wanted his own bed in his own house. Dallas told him that he knew he didn't want to go to the hospital but he really needed to listen to me and trust me that this was the best thing to do right now. John agreed with Dallas as I called for an ambulance. John and Jimmy arrived home and I told them that "Dad was dying and needed to go to the hospital."

The ambulance crew arrived and quickly, efficiently prepared John for transport to St. Luke's. Dallas asked me, "Should we pray?" and we did. We held hands and prayed that God would watch over John and guide the doctors to do whatever they could to keep him with us. Then Dallas drove off while I made my way to the hospital.

The doctors at St. Luke's stabilized John with IV fluids and drained his bladder with a catheter. He was severely dehydrated, but thankfully was responding to their treatments. I sat by his bedside in the emergency room and stared at the floor. I quietly took in our surroundings and watched his chest move up and down as he slept. I listened to the blips of the monitor and watched the lines and numbers on the machine. I looked again at the floor, making pictures in my mind of the pattern in the wood grain. I kept seeing the same picture on the floor over and over; a pattern that resembled a Biblical figure in a robe and holding a shepherd's crook. The Lamb of God who takes away the sins of the world. Jesus was right there with us. I felt strangely comforted. Then I saw something sparkling on the floor. I tried to ignore it but my eyes kept coming back to it. I finally reached down to pick it up. It was a diamond earring, obviously left over from some previous occupant of this room. I picked it up and placed it in my change purse. A diamond represents forever, I thought. We would be together forever.

John was finally transported to a room where I stayed through the night with him. I told the nurses that I was hoping he would be transported by ambulance to Hershey the next day. The nurses didn't think that would happen because the hospitals usually don't do things that way. I was concerned but determined that this time an exception would be made. I called Pastor Doug to let him know that we were back in the hospital.

Pastor Doug came the next day prepared for the worst. He spoke gently to me about the plans God had for us and was glad to hear that I was leaving our fate in God's hands. While Pastor Doug was there, the nurse came in and announced the good news that arrangements were being made for transport to Hershey within the hour.

Pastor Doug said goodbye to John as the ambulance crew prepared him for transport. I suppose Pastor Doug wondered if that was the last time he would see John alive. Perhaps he would be helping me plan a funeral the next time we met. But God was not finished with us yet. He had much work to do to prepare us for the miracle that would unfold in the near future. I quickly drove home and packed the few things I would need for what I thought would be a short stay at Hershey.

Our New Home

As I drew closer to Hershey Medical Center the building shone like a beacon of hope on the horizon. I felt strangely comforted as I found a place to park, quickly making my way to the emergency department where I found John. He was admitted to a room on the 5th floor where the transplant patients stayed. The nurses and staff there are specially trained to deal with the many complex issues related to transplant patients. Dr. Riley checked on John. I gave him a quick update and told him that John was unable to keep anything down, even his medicines. I told Dr. Riley that I suspected hepatic encephalopathy was at the root of this in-ability to swallow, contrary to what the folks at St. Luke's had thought. Dr. Riley told me that I was exactly right. I was relieved to know that the doctors here were on the right track to treat John's condition. Dr. Riley told us that John would need lactulose enemas to get the excess ammonia out of his system.

The nurses found a cot for me to sleep on next to John's bed. They showed me where to find sheets, blankets and anything else I needed to make my stay more comfortable. I settled in and made a tour of my surroundings where I found my way to the cafeteria, coffee and gift shops and the chapel. This busy yet comforting place would become my new home for the next 35 days.

One of the nurses came to our room with John's first lactulose enema. She positioned John on his side. In his weakened condition he tried his best to be a good patient, and a good patient he was. He never complained, and the nurses loved him. This sweet young nurse prepared John for his medicine as I watched her quietly and dutifully do her work. She held one hand on the enema apparatus and struggled with the other hand to hold the bag of lactulose in an upright position. Perhaps I could be of some help. I donned a pair of gloves and held up the bag of syrupy liquid. I told her to tell me when to squeeze the bag. She was very grateful for the help.

It was like trying to squeeze molasses through a straw to direct it to its reluctant destination. This ritual needed to be repeated every two hours, and it worked like a charm. Over the next few days the ammonia made its way out of John's system and he became more alert, though still very weak.

John had developed a cough. The doctors were concerned about fluid building up in his lungs. He would need more attention than the nurses on the 5th floor were able to provide. The plan was to move him to an intermediate unit on the 2nd floor where he would receive more one on one nursing. I packed my few things, folded up my cot and found my way to our "new digs" on the 2nd floor. I would miss the friends we had made on the 5th floor but they assured us that we would see them again soon.

While we were still on the 5th floor, a chaplain came to visit us. John was so weak and his coordination was so poor that he was unable to swallow, even his medicines. It just happened to be Good Friday. John had asked the chaplain if he could serve communion to us. It has been our custom of partaking of the Lord's Supper in reflection of what that day represents. The chaplain was happy to accommodate us and went to the cafeteria for the elements. He brought back some saltine crackers and some grape juice. Together we prayed as he blessed the elements. I was afraid John would choke, not being able to swallow anything. But the Lord knew his heart. He prayed and swallowed the elements without even so much as a cough.

Our room on the 2nd floor was clean, quiet and comfortable and the nurses were every bit as compassionate and friendly as the ones on the 5th floor. They were happy to have me rooming in with John. They showed me how to roll him over often to prevent bedsores. They showed me how to loosen any mucous that might be building up in his lungs by pounding lightly on his back while he lay on his side. I watched how they changed the sheets while he was still in the bed and how they bathed him. I learned quickly and within a few days I was able to do these things by myself.

The nurses were very willing to help but I felt that I needed to learn how so that I could care for him once we were at home. They continued to be understanding and helpful.

The 2nd floor unit rooms were arranged parallel to a circular hallway. While John slept I would often stroll the hallway for a change of scenery and light conversation with the nurses. In the room next to John's lay a small figure surrounded by machinery to monitor his vital signs and help him breathe. I glanced into this room every time I walked by and never saw bright lights on or even another person visiting. One day I walked by and noticed the room was empty. I asked the nurse what had happened to the person in that room and she told me that he had passed away. "Oh, I'm sorry." I exclaimed. "How old was he?" "Fifty two" she answered. I was astonished and said "That's so young!" "Actually" she said, "That's pretty old for a person with Down's Syndrome." I was tempted to ask her what they did with his liver but I kept quiet. Inwardly I was becoming like a buzzard circling its prey for the next "opportunity".

Stress and adversity play strange tricks on the human condition. With each passing day I was developing a macabre sense of humor which was helping me to keep my sanity. I had TV and newspapers and I was able to keep up with what was going on in the world around me. One morning I made my usual trip to the nurses' desk to retrieve the daily newspaper. I looked forward to reading the articles, advice columns, comics and most of all, the puzzle page which kept my wit sharp. In the news this particular morning was a story of the first ever, face transplant. The word "transplant" caught my eye. When the nurse came in to tend to John I asked her if she had seen the article. She hadn't. I gave her a quick description of the story and told her I wondered how they determined a person's placement on the face transplant list. I suppose you would have to be really good looking to be a donor, and really ugly to make the top of the recipient list. We laughed and shared this with some other nurses. It lightened the burden that day.

The Transplant Doctors

Dr. Schreibman came to visit. He told us that John would have the scan of his liver as planned. In the next few days he would meet with the transplant selection committee to determine the urgency for John's need for a new liver. "He's very, very sick." Dr. Schreibman would sadly shake his head and say, but we knew God was in control. John and I prayed often between the tests, treatments and doctor visits.

Shortly after Dr. Schriebman finished with us we were greeted by a small band of doctors. The gentle Japanese doctor stood before us, bowed slightly and announced, "We are transplant surgeons." "Welcome!" I answered as I shook hands with Dr. Uemura. "Are we glad to meet you!" He was accompanied by a tall, big boned Indian man named Dr. Shah and the familiar head of transplant surgery, Dr. Kadry. There were a few other doctors with them but I don't remember their names. They examined John, asked us a few questions and promised to see us again very soon. The journey toward a new liver had begun.

The final hurdle was for John to have the CT scan which would reveal the status of his liver tumors. Every day we prayed that the tumors would not show any new activity. If the scan showed what the doctors had hoped for John would be placed at the top of the transplant list at Hershey.

Meanwhile the plan of treatment was for John to be able to receive some nourishment to make him strong enough to survive the surgery. Being unable to swallow made that extremely difficult. A feeding tube was inserted into his nose, which led down into his stomach. Liquid nourishment was then hooked up to the feeding tube. "Liquid potato chips!" I would tell John in an effort to keep him cheerful.

While napping on my cot next to John's bed one afternoon I woke up to find him tugging at his nose while asleep. To my horror, he had accidentally pulled out the feeding tube. I called for the nurse to come and see. She brought one of the transplant residents along with her, and they tried to re-insert the tube. By this time John was awake. Each time they tried to re-insert the tube, it would bunch up in his throat and they would have to pull it back out. Dr. Shah came into the room and asked what was going on. I was a little scared of this big, serious looking man. I was afraid that he would be annoyed at the fact that John had pulled the tube out but I had to tell him the truth. I told Dr. Shah that John had his hand to his face while sleeping and didn't realize he had pulled the tube out. "Let me try." Dr. Shah said as he opened a new tube kit. "Well, if you can transplant a liver, I suppose you can put a hose in the nose!" I exclaimed. Dr. Shah smiled. He told John to open his mouth and he gently threaded the tube into John's nose. Each time John opened his mouth his tongue would automatically go up in the roof of his mouth, blocking the view of his throat. I noticed a jar of tongue depressors sitting on the counter by the window along with a flashlight. I took a tongue depressor out of the jar, held John's tongue down with it and aimed the lit flashlight into his throat with the other hand. Now Dr. Shah had two free hands to do his work and light to see where the tube was going. The tube went right down. "Nice working with you!" Dr. Shah said to me. "You could be a good assistant." I liked Dr. Shah from that moment on. To this day he is our favorite, and he says that's because he's bigger than everyone else.

Listed!!

The Day had finally arrived! Dr. Schreibman came to visit us with good news. The CT scan had showed no new tumor activity. Now it was time for Dr. Schreibman to meet with the transplant selection committee in the hope of convincing them that John was a good candidate for surgery. He was cautiously optimistic but warned me that the surgeons might feel that John was too sick to survive the surgery. That being said, Dr. Schreibman left the room to go and meet with the committee. His words hung on my heart and mind as I sat there for a moment trying to digest all that had just been said.

I hurried to the hallway and stopped him. "Dr. Schreibman!" I called out. He stopped and turned. "Please make them understand." I pleaded, "I know how very sick John is, but without the surgery he WILL die." Dr. Schreibman understood what I was saying but he gently explained to me that if they went ahead and did the surgery on someone too weak, the person would die and the transplant committee would feel that they had wasted the organ. "Oh, no." I answered, "Where there's life there's hope. Please don't let them give up on us." Dr. Schreibman gently took me by the shoulders and said, "Mrs. Ellermann. Don't worry. Let me do the worrying for you." He sounded so confident, and yet so gentle.

Dr. Schreibman was not able to see us personally later on that day but at 4:30PM John's room telephone rang. Dr. Schreibman reported the good news that John had been listed status 1-A. He would see us tomorrow morning. John slept peacefully while I lay on the cot and quietly thanked God. Months later I was told how passionately Dr. Schreibman had advocated on our behalf. He was very happy that he would not be faced with giving us bad news. Somehow he knew that we were not prepared to take "no" for an answer.

The next morning Dr. Schreibman came to visit as promised. He explained to us, "Now comes the hard part; waiting for a liver." I answered, "Are you kidding? The hard part was getting listed!" He agreed that getting listed was a real challenge but it may take up to six months to get a liver. We may get called multiple times before they actually find one that is a good match. Some people even die while waiting for a liver. It will be an emotional roller coaster and we will have to be very patient. I assured Dr. Schreibman that we were up to the challenge. "Now, I'll be gone for two weeks." He explained, "Dr. Riley will be seeing you during that time. If you are still here when I get back, I'll see you then. If not, I'll see you in clinic." We thanked him again and said goodbye.

Dr. Riley watched over John during those next two weeks. During that time we were faced with some new challenges. John's kidneys were beginning to shut down and he would need to be placed on dialysis. That was known as Hepato-renal Syndrome. The sick liver tells the kidneys "we don't need you anymore so you can just shut down now and go to sleep." John now needed dialysis three times a week to keep his kidneys functioning. Dr. Riley explained to me that if John needed dialysis for more than eight weeks he would probably need a kidney as well as a liver. "Where will we get that?" I asked in a panic. "We're having a hard enough time getting a liver!" "Oh, that's not a problem." Dr. Riley assured me. "The kidneys come with it." I was amazed! "You're kidding!" I exclaimed. "Like a burger and fries?" "Exactly." Dr. Riley answered. "Like a value meal." John didn't need the value meal after all. Some other fortunate recipient got the "fries"; John got the "burger."

During that same two week period John had two offers for a liver; both of which were not a good match. Dr. Schreibman was amazed when he came back that John had already had two offers. His MELD score had reached as high as 39 on a scale of 6 through 40. Dr. Schreibman reasoned that John had the "eye of the tiger" watching out for him. He was hopeful for us and eager to see that John would get a liver soon.

Visits and Phone Calls

Yvonne called my cell phone. "Would you like some company?" she asked. I was thrilled! Her son, Chris, who is a truck driver, had agreed to make the trip with her from Southern New Jersey. It would have been a very difficult trip for her to make alone. I had never thought of the possibility of her being able to visit because of the distance involved. I had settled for being content with phone calls and e-mails. Now it would be wonderful to be able to visit in person.

It had been a busy morning on the second floor. In addition to the usual duties required of staff, there had been a "code blue" drill. I don't know much about these drills but I assume they are a "dress rehearsal" for the actual emergency. Everyone moves quickly and efficiently when this happens.

Yvonne and Chris arrived in the early afternoon. John was very weak that day. I had updated Yvonne on his latest condition when she had arrived. She had not seen John for a handful of months now. I, on the other hand had been living day to day with seeing John's loss of weight, muscle tone and sickly complexion.

Yvonne was shocked when she saw John but she tried hard not to show it. John could barely talk to her between coughs and gags. We made him comfortable for a nap and

I suggested we go to the cafeteria for a snack. Perhaps being out of the room for awhile would help her to deal with the shock of what she had just seen.

The three of us walked to the hallway and waited for the elevator while I tried to make casual conversation. The door opened and Yvonne told me she felt queasy. With that, her eyes rolled up and she fainted right there in the hallway! Chris had caught her and lowered her to the floor while I peeked around the corner and asked for assistance. The person who I asked for assistance pressed the "code" button. Nurses and doctors came running! They were pumped from the earlier drill! Yvonne woke up to find a large group of people in white medical coats standing over her. "Oh my God!" She said. "What happened?" "You fainted." I told her. "Here is the entire staff of Hershey Medical Center. Now, aren't you impressed?"

Someone brought us a wheelchair and Chris and I took Yvonne to the emergency room. I am happy to say that all checked out good. The emergency room doctors felt it was a reaction to seeing John in his deteriorated condition. Yvonne felt bad and apologized for the commotion. She felt guilty because she wanted to comfort me and here I wound up comforting her. That was ok, I assured her. The distraction was good for me. I was beginning to find that the more I reached out to someone with an urgent need the more comforting it was to me.

A few days later John's oldest son, Matthew called from Montana. I had been regularly updating Matthew on John's condition. The latest was the good news that John had been upgraded to the top of the transplant list. John seemed very calm that day, but sleepy. He had been unaware of the many conversations taking place between family members to update them on his condition. I put the phone to John's ear so he could say hello to Matthew. John was happy to hear Matthew's voice but suddenly remembered him as a little boy. He asked Matthew, "When you come out can you bring the Pooh Bear book and read it to me? I always loved when you would read that book?" I could only imagine what poor Matthew was thinking on the other end of the phone. 'This is how people talk when they are dying. Will I ever see Dad again?' I had to talk to Matthew and assure him that John was as stable as could be expected and the doctors were hoping for a good outcome. I took the phone and went to the hallway where I explained to Matthew the tricks that liver disease play on the mind. I wanted to cry for Matthew that day. He must have been terrified.

Jimmy and John had been keeping the home fires burning and had also been updated on a regular basis regarding their dad's condition. From their standpoint it did not sound like things were going well. They tried hard to go about their daily business of making life seem normal, but there were days when things really looked grim. On this particular night they sat in their "man cave" discussing what would become of us all if something were to happen to Dad. They both cried. If I had known this I would have been heartbroken as well at the prospect of not being able to be there to comfort them. But God knew they needed someone to comfort them, so He sent them an angel. Her name is Michelle.

John's new girlfriend was on hand that night to comfort and cheer both of them. From then on she would often stay at the house and help with the everyday chores that two young men often take for granted. She would send me cheerful text messages with the latest updates from home. I would tell her how I missed my cats and she would send pictures via phone. I could hold that little cell phone in my hand and enjoy a little piece of "normal" from home.

Three months later I rejoiced one day while rooming in with John at Hershey for subsequent hernia surgery. Our son, John had sent me a text message from his cell phone which read "We need to find a promise ring for Michelle. This one's a keeper!" We are so happy to have this young woman in our lives. She is truly family to us.

5th *Floor . . . Welcome Back*

John seemed to be responding well to dialysis. He was now stable enough to be moved back to the 5th floor. We were both happy about that and looked forward to seeing the nurses who had taken such good care of him when we had first arrived. We would miss our friends from the second floor but they were happy as well. Fifth floor meant you were getting better and were not quite as sick.

Arrangements were made for John to have a dialysis port inserted in his chest so that he could receive dialysis on a regular basis, three times a week. Jimmy, John and two friends had come to visit shortly before John was scheduled to have his dialysis port inserted. The procedure would not take long. John was wheeled away for the procedure while I went to the cafeteria to entertain his visitors. We had our snack, said our goodbyes and then I returned to John's room. Just in time. He was being brought back from the procedure. His face looked purple! The doctors tried to wake him up but couldn't. I was in a panic and feared the worst. I called John and Jimmy. They immediately turned around and drove back to the hospital. To us it appeared as though John had a stroke, but what had actually happened was that his liver could no longer process the anesthesia that he was given for the insertion of the dialysis port. He was brought back to the second floor again where it took two days for the anesthesia to work its way out of his system. I was beginning to wonder if we would ever get out of here. Would life ever become "normal" again? Would I ever be able to get back to managing my household and looking after my whole family? I missed those normal things.

At least I had my laptop computer and I could connect with friends through e-mail and facebook. I checked those things on a daily basis. I would see the daily posts from John's friend, Frank who was the Eminent Commander of Allen-Beauceant Knights Templar Commandery this year, where John and Frank both were members.

Frank would call me every day and ask of the latest news of John. He had been worried when he had seen John at his worst a month ago at home. Frank was very concerned for me as well. Now he would often encourage me with moral support and post the latest news of our progress on his facebook page for everyone to see.

One morning I checked the facebook wall and found that our son, John had written, 'My mom sits by my dad's bedside day and night tending to his every need. She never leaves his side. This is what true love really is.' I cried tears of Joy that day and I still do as I write this, knowing that God has given me the opportunity to teach our sons what true love is really about. There are blessings that come to us in our darkest moments.

In the midst of this chaos we were visited a few times by a young chaplain. He may have told us his name but neither one of us remembered. Strangely enough though, we remembered every other detail about him. He was tall, thin, with a short haircut and wore a pale green shirt that made his hazel eyes appear mostly green. He reminded us of our Jimmy. He had a gentle voice and would often sing songs to us that he had learned at church youth camp. He prayed with us often and nicknamed John, "John the Beloved." He seemed to show up whenever we urgently needed someone to pray with.

Fortunately, John's stay on the second floor was short. Once again he was moved to the fifth floor. We knew that this time the next step was "home!" We waited patiently in anticipation while arrangements were made for John to have dialysis three times a week near our home.

John was very weak, and the doctors were concerned that I would not be able to manage getting him in and out of the house. His blood work could be done by a visiting nurse, but what about dialysis? They suggested we think about short term rehab, but I was determined to try first. The day finally came when they felt he was stable enough to return home and wait for a liver.

The nurses reviewed John's discharge instructions with me and I helped him to get dressed. I made him comfortable in a hospital recliner while we waited for someone from transport to arrive with a wheelchair. Once the wheelchair had arrived we discovered we could not get John out of the recliner. He was dead weight and ended up on the floor as we tried to lift him. We would not be going home today after all.

Short Term Rehab

A social worker was assigned to find a short term rehab for John near our home. The doctors were concerned that it would at this point be impossible for me to care for John on my own since he was so weak. He would need skilled nurses to care for him round the clock.

The social worker came to our room with all the necessary paperwork to get things started. She was a delightful woman. A big smile, cute little dreadlocks and a great sense of humor. I joked with Lina, and she laughed while John looked on in amusement. Lina made the idea of a short term rehab sound like an acceptable solution to our current dilemma. It had its advantages. John would be in a comfortable bed, near a bathroom, and all of his meals would be prepared the way he needed them. Perhaps this would work out well and he would get stronger and be better able to withstand surgery when the time came. He would also be near home so that I could tend to things at home and at the same time get some much needed rest. This could turn out to be a good thing, I had hoped.

I told Lina that I would have to check out the rehab center in person before agreeing to have John transported there. I drove home and checked on the house. Yes, it was still standing, and everything was in its place too. Then I drove to the address of the rehab center. It was a beautiful place. It was impeccably clean and I had come at the right time. They were planning a spaghetti dinner for a fundraiser that very evening. Dallas and I attended and met some very nice people. We had a chance to mingle with some of the residents who all seemed to be very happy there. There were even volunteers involved who John and I had known from church.

I met the director who gave me a quick tour of the facility. I took some pictures so that John could see them. I was introduced to some of the nurses and volunteers. The assisted living section was particularly beautiful and the grounds were picturesque.

The facility was surrounded by individual housing specially designed for senior living. This was a community within. If John and I were by ourselves I would consider living there. It was delightful, and I told the director we would be checking John in soon.

The next day, May 5th to be exact, arrangements were made to transport John by ambulance to the rehab facility. I knew that I could not room in with him there but I could stay all day from 8AM until 10PM, and even later if needed. If any problem occurred regarding his condition I could be called in the middle of the night and would be allowed to stay with John.

John was assigned to a semi-private room, and once settled, was given a wheelchair tour of the facility and grounds by the director. He enjoyed the tour and was pleased with his new surroundings. Then we returned to his room. His room mate was a frail looking man who appeared to have had a stroke. The man had difficulty speaking and was not able to carry on a conversation but was able to communicate through gestures.

John's clothes were unpacked and labeled with his name and room number. I arranged his clothes in the dresser and closet. Then we made an inventory of his toiletries in the bathroom. There was a place for everything.

John sat in the wheelchair while the nurse explained to us that if he wanted to get in or out of bed he would need to call for assistance because they didn't want him to fall. She showed him the call button on his wheelchair and the one near the bed. She explained that if he were to get out of bed on his own, an alarm would go off that would send staff to investigate it's cause. 'Hmm.' I thought, 'this could be a problem' but resigned myself to being compliant.

There was one tv in the room. "Suppose one wants to watch TV and the other one doesn't?" I asked, "and suppose one wants to watch a certain program?" "You just have to compromise" the nurse answered, "that's how we do it." I thought this was a little unusual. Even in a semi-private hospital room there is one TV per patient. I had planned on John using TV earphones when he wanted to watch a certain program. I supposed we would have to adjust. The nurse left to allow us to familiarize ourselves with the new surroundings.

Fifteen minutes later John told me he needed to use the bathroom. I told him to use the call button and we would wait for the nurse. The nurses here seemed to discourage my trying on my own to help John with these everyday tasks. It's different than the hospital. The reason for that being that everything is about liability. Nobody wants to be sued because a resident fell. We waited and waited for the nurse. No one came. John told me again he really needed to go, so I helped him out of the wheelchair and into the bathroom as I had been used to doing. The nurse finally came. I told her that I realized they must be awfully busy so I helped John myself. Everything was fine now. Secretly I thought, 'If you're gonna insist on helping him, you're gonna have to move faster than this, honey. Lactulose works quickly!' I didn't dare say what I was thinking. I didn't want them labeling John 'difficult'.

I stayed with John for the remainder of the day. We had arrived too late for the big meal of the day. He was given a sandwich around suppertime which he ate a few bites of. He enjoyed the fruit punch and had more than one glass of that. The nurses tucked him into bed and he tried his best to get comfortable. We had noticed that whenever the man in the next bed moved around too much, the bed alarm sounded, sending nurses to investigate. John was worried that if he needed to move around his alarm would sound too. I peeked under the sheets, then the mattress and found the alarm connection. I discreetly unplugged the alarm and tucked the wires underneath the mattress. Problem solved! I hoped John would get a good night's sleep. I kissed him goodnight, armed him with his cell phone just in case he needed me, and told him I would be back first thing in the morning.

I stopped at the nurses' desk to say goodnight. The nurses were in the process of changing shifts and wanted the on-coming shift to review John's medications with me. "Why is he taking xifaxin?" They asked. "That's used for traveler's diaharrea." I explained to them how xifaxin removes toxins from the intestines and at the same time prevents diaharrea. I also explained how important it was that John be given his medications when needed and went on to explain what each medicine was for. The nurses listened intently. Those who weren't even assigned to John stopped to listen and were very interested in what I was saying. They began to ask questions. "Is he number one on the whole transplant list in the whole country?" They asked increduously. "How many people are on the list?"

I dove into my explanation of all I had learned about liver transplant. "No, he is not number one in the whole country" I explained. "Although he IS number one in MY book!" They laughed. "There are 17,000 people on the list right now for a liver." I went on to explain, "John is number one in region two which consists of all of PA, NJ, Delaware, West Virginia and Washington, DC." They were amazed! They had a celebrity in their midst. Now they wanted to know even more of what they could do to help. "Tell us more about his condition." They said with eagerness in their voices. I explained the complications of liver disease and they were equally amazed that I knew so much. I had been taught well by the doctors at Hershey and was beginning to sound like Dr. Schreibman. "Any questions?" I ended my "lecture" with. I then instructed them to call me immediately if they received a call from Hershey Medical Center regarding a liver for John.

They were so excited to be a part of this history being made! They had never had a transplant patient before. They were not to attempt to make arrangements for John to be transported to Hershey. I would take him there myself so that we could arrive with all of the necessary paperwork which I regularly kept in my possession. I then left in hopes of getting a good night's sleep for the first time in I couldn't remember when.

I had been instructed that John would be given breakfast, medications and then taken to physical therapy which would last for about two hours. I had been informed that in a few days the director would meet with the staff to go over his plan of care. I had been invited to sit in on this meeting and offer whatever input would be helpful to them. It seemed the appropriate time for me to arrive to spend time with John each day would be around noontime. On the days he had dialysis he would be transported to a nearby dialysis facility around 11AM.

John was happy to see me. Dallas came to visit too. John asked Dallas if he and I could have a few minutes together to discuss something private. "Sure." Dallas answered, and then walked down the hallway to chat with the nurses. John wanted to go someplace where we could be alone so I wheeled him to the end of the hallway; a quiet place with a big picture window and a lovely view. I sat down on the window ledge to face him. He burst into tears and told me, "If you love me, you'll get me out of here." I was horrified! "What happened?" I asked. "Is there a problem with your room mate?"

His room mate wasn't the problem. It seems that during the night he had to use the bathroom. He rang for the nurse as instructed. When she arrived she told him that he could not get out of bed and go to the bathroom without wearing slippers. I had placed his slipper socks in the top drawer with all of his other socks. The nurse couldn't find them so she told him to put on his sneakers. He did, and she told him he would have to tie them so that he wouldn't trip on the laces. He was feeling more and more during all this that his need to go was becoming more urgent. He was afraid he would have an accident. But by the time John had finally made it to the bathroom he had lost the urge to go. The nurse stood impatiently by, asking him, "Are you done yet?" He apologized for the inconvenience and she escorted him back to bed.

"I don't belong here." John blurted out. He was right. The average age of the typical patient was about 85 years old, some suffering from mild dementia. John was only 65 and in great shape before liver disease had reared its ugly head. I told John that I would be meeting with the staff and director regarding his care in a few days. If he could hang on until then everything would be ok. I would stay as long as permitted and be with him whenever he didn't have physical therapy or dialysis. We would make sure all of his needs were taken care of before he was tucked into bed for the night and he could call me anytime of night on his cell phone. He calmed down and I told the nurses at the desk that he had been feeling anxious. "We could give him something to calm him down." They assured me. "You are absolutely not to do that." I answered. "Any medications not already on his chart must be cleared with the transplant team at Hershey." I knew now that I could not leave John in the care of these well intentioned, but not well informed caregivers.

After supper the nurses told us they would give John a nice hot shower. I told them to be very careful not to get any water into his dialysis port as we had previously been instructed by the nurses at Hershey. While we were still at Hershey I had given him a shower one afternoon. The nurses there had showed me how to cover up the dialysis port with waterproof bandaging. They had used a clear plastic covering with a sticky edge to cover up the port. I asked the nurses at the rehab center if they had any waterproof bandaging and they said no. One of them appeared in the doorway with some large gauze pads but I explained that wouldn't do. Water would get onto the gauze pad and seep right into the port. "How about some saran wrap from the kitchen?" I suggested. "Bring me some of that, and some medical tape too." The young nurse eagerly dashed off to complete her mission while we dressed John in a hospital gown for his trip to the shower at the end of the hallway.

We covered the port in saran wrap and carefully taped the edges. "Water may still seep in." the nurse worried. "Do you have a hand held shower head?" I asked, to which she answered, "yes". "Then it will be no problem." I told her. "Just guide the shower head here below the port and no water will get in." "Do you want to come with us?" She asked. "I think I'd better." I reasoned.

We wheeled John down the hallway in his portable "shower chair" to the shower room. Once inside, he was positioned in a stall, the gown was removed and he was "hosed down." The whole experience was degrading to say the least. The only good part about this was that everything smelled nice when the procedure was done. My mind had been made up. I would tell the staff at the up-coming meeting that John would not be staying here. All they were doing could be done for John at home by me.

I stayed with John as often as possible each day. Perhaps a change of scenery would help John to feel more "normal."

We planned on having dinner in the dining room instead of John's room. John was assigned a seat at a table with a few of the other residents. The dining area was cheerful and elegant and I hoped we would enjoy our dinner. That was not to be. John took one bite of his dinner and threw up. I quickly grabbed a teacup for him to throw up into. He was very embarrassed, so I wheeled him back to his room.

John drank fruit punch, for which I was grateful. He wasn't getting much nourishment but at least he was getting liquid and wouldn't dehydrate. I stayed until bedtime and told John I would see him tomorrow. I tried to sleep at home in my own bed but sleep wouldn't come to my tired body. My mind raced to thoughts of how many days it would be until I could bring John home where he would be safe and comfortable. I tossed and turned in bed and glanced at the clock. 3AM and still no sleep.

My cell phone rang. Oh, no! It was John. I hoped nothing was wrong. "Can you come over?" he asked. "They will let you in. It's real important." "Did something happen?" I asked. "No." he said, "but I have something real important to tell you." "Can it wait until morning?" I asked. "It's only a few hours until 8:00 and maybe you can tell me then." "Ok" he answered in an annoyed tone. "If you don't want to hear about it then I'm sorry I bothered you." I couldn't let the rest of the night go by without hearing what John had to say. There was no point in staying here trying to get some sleep. Sleep would not come unless my mind was at ease.

I pulled on some clothes, staggered out to my car and drove to the rehab center. All was quiet. The whole world was asleep except for me. I tiptoed quietly to the entrance and rang the bell. I explained to the night shift nurse that John had called me and I needed to see him. Quietly and discreetly I slipped into his room, and he was glad to see me. "Can we go someplace and talk?" he whispered. I helped him to his wheelchair and steered him to the comfortable, pristine reception area.

I'm "glad you came." He told me, "I have good news! I've been cured! I don't need a new liver!" "Are you sure?" I asked him, suspecting his ammonia level was playing tricks on his brain again. "You believe me, don't you?" he asked. "I hope it's true." I answered. "Well, that's good news. How about if we get you back to bed and I'll be back in a few hours, ok?" John was satisfied with my answer and went along with my suggestions. I drove back home, slept for an hour and returned to the rehab for "round three."

I expected to find John wide awake and eager to see me but instead he was lethargic and sleepy. I suspected his ammonia level was on the rise since the strange encounter during the night. I advised the nurses of this and they were perplexed. "What should we do?" they asked. "You have to give him an extra dose of lactulose." I explained. "But his chart says 3 times a day and we have already given him two doses."

I asked them if they had any insulin dependent diabetic patients in their care. "Yes, we do." They answered. "What do you do when their blood sugar is high?" I asked. "We give them extra insulin." They answered. "Lactulose works the same way." I explained. "When the patient seems lethargic or confused you give them an extra dose of lactulose to lower the ammonia in their system. It's very important to keep the ammonia level down. If the ammonia level gets too high

118

the person will go into a coma and die." "We can't give him extra medicine without the doctor's orders." They told me, "and the doctor only comes once a week." "OK. I'll tell you what." I had an idea. "Pour a dose of lactulose and bring it to me. I'll give it to him. That way you won't be blamed." Knowing that the doctor was not available on a moment's notice, they complied. It helped. By early evening John was thinking clearly again.

I needed to do all that I could to keep John's spirits up. I knew how lonely he was when I was unable to be there with him at night, and my heart would break when I thought of how he must miss us, and our cats too. We could come and visit, but what about the cats? People do bring their pets to visit residents in nursing homes. Perhaps I could bring John's favorite of our three cats, Taco B.

I inquired at the nurses' desk and they agreed. Everyone loved Taco. She is a beautiful cat. She is white, orange and black calico with big round eyes and a plump figure. Early on she had "adopted" John as her very own. She would climb onto his lap and knead, exactly where his liver was located. I had even used my camera to make a video of her doing it. I showed it to Dr. Cornell and announced that we were participating in an experimental cancer treatment called "felo-therapy." Unlike traditional chemo, it has no negative side effects. Actually the experience is quite pleasant. Dr. Cornell was amused. He loved cats and wondered why they do that. I am somewhat of an expert on cats. I have raised them since I was 6 years old. I explained that when they knead it reminds them of when they were nursing kittens. They do that to the mother cat's belly which helps stimulate the milk supply.

Taco B. was happy to see her daddy. It didn't matter that there was an unfamiliar bed. She curled up next to him and purred. Soon she was asleep. At last, there was something "normal" from home to comfort John.

May 9th, that Sunday was a day we had all been waiting for. John's friends and fellow fire company members had planned a benefit breakfast in his honor. John was well enough to attend. I arrived at the rehab facility early that morning where they had John all ready to attend his benefit breakfast. Many of our friends throughout the community showed up at the fire company, along with members of our church and neighboring fire companies. Over 600 people were in attendance and over $6,000 was raised for John. That money was enough to pay for his entire first year of anti-rejection medications which he would need for the rest of his life once he received his new liver.

John was happy to see all of his friends. He ate a small but significant portion of breakfast and did so well with it that I decided to take him to church. People flocked to greet him in church and we cried tears of joy to be in the Lord's house together on this beautiful Sunday morning. It was Mother's Day, and this was my gift. What a perfect Mother's Day it was turning out to be! Next we drove by the house. Every inch of my being ached to get John out of the car and bring him inside but I didn't dare. The thought of having to bring him back to rehab would be too painful for both of us. We admired our house from the driveway and then made the short trip back to rehab.

The nurses were worried. We had been gone well past our curfew of 11AM. It was now 2:30. The staff were kind and understanding when I reported that John had done so well that I took him to church. There was church in the afternoon at rehab too. John wanted to attend, so I wheeled him to the church service area where we met a minister from a local church. John told him that he was active in his own church and offered to participate in the service. I was so proud of John. As sick as he was he made it to the pulpit for the Bible reading. He read from the Word as God smiled down on us from above.

I wheeled John back to his room. We had company. Dallas was there, and Jimmy along with his friend, John Grantz. Grantz had been helping our sons to keep up with the daily tasks of caring for the house and had come along on several visits to Hershey. We were all enjoying a good visit when my cell phone rang. It was Hershey. They wanted John to come. They had a call for a liver and they wanted him prepped and ready. "Ask for a cardboard box and pack all of John's things in it. Bring it all to the house." I instructed Dallas. "We're leaving." I thanked the nurses and staff for their hospitality and whisked John off to Hershey. Perhaps this would be the perfect ending to the perfect day.

False Alarm

We arrived at Hershey Medical Center within two hours of the phone call. John was admitted to a room on the 5th floor where our friends, the transplant nurses had been eagerly awaiting his arrival. My cot was waiting for me outside of our assigned room. By this time we all knew the drill. The nurses began doing all that was necessary to prepare John for the possibility of surgery, which included collecting seventeen tubes of blood for the purpose of cross matching him for a new liver.

Dr. Kadry and Dr. Uemura stopped in to inform us of the latest progress in hopes of surgery. We waited in anticipation of the promised good news. The hours crept by slowly while we tried to remain calm by watching TV or napping. Early evening soon became midnight, and midnight, almost dawn. We listened as the medi-vac hovered above the building. Perhaps it contained the precious cargo we so eagerly awaited, but no one came to bring us the news we had hoped for.

Finally, in mid morning on May 10th Dr. Kadry came to see us. "I'm afraid you won't be getting this liver, Mr. Ellermann" she informed us. "You see, there is a man in the ICU who is very sick and is at the top of the list." We had remembered how Dr. Schreibman had warned us that this may happen, even several times. "It looks like you will have to return to rehab." Dr. Kadry explained. "I'm afraid that's out of the question." I answered Dr. Kadry. "I had John's belongings removed when we left there and I told them we wouldn't be back." Dr. Kadry was concerned that John was not strong enough to be cared for at home. Perhaps he would fall or have to go up and down steps many times during the day. I explained that we lived in a bi-level house where all that we needed was on the upper level. Our bedroom, bathroom and kitchen were all on that floor, and once I had John inside the house, this is where we would stay. Jimmy and John could help me to get him into the house once we had arrived at home. I would even make arrangements to have a stair lift installed so that I could get John back and forth to dialysis.

Dr. Kadry seemed doubtful that I could handle all of this, but I knew how John felt about going back to rehab. I asked Dr. Kadry if she felt it was important that a patient be emotionally strong to survive a liver transplant.

"Absolutely. That is just as important as being physically strong enough." She answered. "I thought so too." I agreed, and explained to her that John was very unhappy at rehab even though it was such a beautiful facility. If he were forced to return there it would break his spirit, thus making him unfit for surgery. I could easily do everything that was being done for him at rehab. "Well" Dr. Kadry agreed, "Let's get someone from physical therapy to see how John can manage with a walker and a few steps."

Perfect timing! The physical therapist arrived as we were speaking. She adjusted a walker for John's height and we walked alongside him as he strolled the hallway with his newfound "best friend", the walker. We walked to the end of the hallway where there was a staircase. John practiced using the steps as the therapist instructed me on how to guide him from alongside just in case he began to lose his balance. He did very well, and so did I.

We heard footsteps in the stairway. Fast footsteps as if someone were almost running up the stairs. Dr. Uemura appeared in the stairway, headed toward the fifth floor. "Hey!" I greeted him. "What happened to that liver you promised us? You were supposed to put his name on it." He smiled and answered, "Next time! Next time! Liver for you." And in the blink of an eye he disappeared. Busy doctors!

John was discharged later that day. By early evening he was comfortable in his own bed as I snuggled up next to him. 'God has blessed us'. I thought. We basked in our familiar surroundings and enjoyed the company of our sons, their friends, and our cats. All was well. We could wait.

Dialysis

John had been scheduled for dialysis in a free standing clinic three times a week. Thanks to the expertise of the physical therapists at Hershey, I was able to get him down the steps, out of the house, into the car and back home again without any problems. I had made arrangements with a local company who sold and installed stair lifts. The cost would be around $3,000 which I could take from our savings. The stair lift would be installed next week. In the meantime we would manage. This was not as difficult as I had thought it would be.

The dialysis clinic was located near the mall. John would be receiving dialysis for about three hours each time we went there. This was almost pleasant. I could browse the shops and bookstores while John had his treatment and return to take him home when his treatment was finished. Other people came to dialysis on the same schedule. Some were quiet, others were more talkative. We didn't converse much in the waiting area but enjoyed listening to the others, some of whom had obviously become close friends. One lady talked of the foods she enjoyed eating, which were considered "no-no's" for anyone on dialysis. The foods she so enjoyed were all loaded with salt.

John hated dialysis but was a real trooper. He had to sit in a recliner for three hours while hooked to machinery that filtered his blood flow through his kidneys. It was always cold in the treatment area. Liver disease makes a person cold to begin with and all John wanted was to be warm and tucked under his covers. The thin blankets provided were not enough to keep him warm. The constant whirr of the machines and the sterile, cold treatment area were hardly a comfortable environment. Three hours, three times a week was more than enough of this, but John never complained.

Blood pressure is continuously monitored during dialysis. John's blood pressure would drop and be considered too low for him to be released to return home. The dialysis nurse called a nephrologist who advised calling an ambulance to take him to St. Luke's emergency room. This happened not once, but twice. I was becoming concerned that something would be done in the emergency room at the advice of this doctor who had never even met John in person. Perhaps the proposed treatment would be in conflict of what would be deemed acceptable by the transplant team at Hershey.

There were now "too many fingers in the pie" I thought. Someone may accidentally compromise John's chances of getting a new liver.

The second time that it was suggested that John be taken to the emergency room I told the nurse that I would take him to Hershey myself. We could not afford to take any chances. He had already had three offers for a liver. The nurse took John's blood pressure again and thankfully it had returned to an acceptable level for us to return home. It seemed as though this would happen each time I took him to dialysis.

May 16th: It's Sunday. The sun is shining and it's a beautiful day but May 16th is always somehow bittersweet to me. It's the anniversary of my father's death. I still miss him as though it were yesterday even though he is gone for twenty two years today. However, the memories of him always bring a smile to my face, along with tears of joy as I remember his sense of humor. I wonder what he would have thought of all this.

John is very uncomfortable today. His belly is swollen and filled with fluid. Tomorrow morning I will take him to St. Luke's for his routine paracentesis procedure where they will drain the excess fluid from his abdomen. I wonder how much fluid they will remove this time. He has dialysis on Tuesday. That also removes some excess fluid. I worry that removal of too much fluid in too short a time span will cause him to dehydrate. What should I do?

Perhaps John will feel more comfortable sitting in his recliner in the living room. I helped him to get out of bed and positioned his walker so that he could make his way to the living room. I am encouraged as I see how well he is able to move with the walker. He sat in his recliner for a short time, trying to be a good sport for as long as his swollen belly would allow. "Maybe I could get him into the car and take him for a ride" I suggested to son, John and Michelle. John thought that would be a good idea, but his belly was so swollen that gravity had won. It took all three of us; our son, Michelle and I to get John out of the recliner. Once we were able to do that I decided to take him to Hershey and explain our plight. We were reaching the point in his illness where everything that needed to be done for him should be done under the watchful eyes of the transplant team. We had come too far for anyone to make a mistake and jeopardize his chance for getting a new liver.

I grabbed my bag of necessary items which I had by now learned to keep packed along with the transplant notebook which had become my "Bible" and we were on our way to "liver-land."

Another Short Vacation In Liver Land

We arrived at the emergency department in Hershey Medical Center in late afternoon. Jason, the transplant resident greeted us and examined John. He made arrangements for John to be admitted so that paracentesis could be done and arranged for the nephrology team to schedule John for dialysis. The nephrologist came to see us in the emergency department. I explained to him that whenever John had dialysis his blood pressure would drop dangerously low, and now his belly would quickly fill with fluid that needed to be drained. I told him that I was concerned about too many doctors treating John who were not familiar with his status on the transplant list. My fear was that someone might make a mistake that would cost John his chance for a new liver.

The nephrologist felt that all of my concerns were valid. I told him that I wanted everything to be done for John here. That made sense to him but he warned me that it would involve a one hundred sixty mile round trip three times a week for us. I would do what had to be done, I told him. I planned to rent an apartment for us close by with a short term lease until that time came when John would receive a new liver. We had money saved for a rainy day and now it was "pouring"! He agreed, and made the necessary arrangements for John to be put on a dialysis schedule at

Hershey. He would be admitted to the fifth floor where by this time we were on a first name basis with the nurses and staff there. They would have my cot ready so that I could once again room in with John.

Then the phone rang. I didn't bother to answer because no one I knew of would be calling me on John's emergency room phone. Jason answered and told me that the call was for me. It was Dr. Kadry. There had been another offer for a liver! She was very happy to hear that we had already arrived and that John was in the process of being admitted. The liver offered was coming from a "high risk" donor, meaning that the donor had been a drug user. There would be a risk of John contracting hepatitis from this new liver but hepatitis could be treated and the benefit of receiving this liver outweighed the risk of waiting for another offer. Who knows how long we would have to wait for another opportunity. We agreed to take the offer, and John was transported to the fifth floor where he would once again be prepped for potential surgery.

The nurses were happy to see us and hopeful that the outcome would be what we were all waiting for. I called John's best friend, Ed. Ed and John had known each other since college days and had been the best of friends for many years. Ed had been the best man when John was married the first time and had stood by us as well. John had also been the best man when Ed married his wife, Ginnie. Ginnie and I had become good friends over the years too, but sadly, Ginnie had passed away from lymphoma in 1994. Ed had been widowed ever since. He was a wonderful husband and father in addition to being a loyal and true friend. He wanted to help us in whatever way he could. I thought surely

131

John would receive a liver this time and wanted someone to keep me company while he was in surgery. Who would be a better choice for that than Ed? He came and stayed all night while we waited for word from the transplant surgeons. Ed tried to sleep in the hospital recliner but could not get comfortable. I felt so bad for him and wished we would hear from the transplant surgeons soon, but the hours crept by while we waited. Nothing happened.

Early the next morning Dr. Kadry came to see us. The news was not what we had hoped for. Someone on the list was in need of a double organ transplant; a heart and a liver which must come from the same donor. When someone needs a double organ transplant they are automatically placed at the top of the list. We would have to wait for another offer once again, but this time John would stay at the hospital. He had already been scheduled for paracentesis that morning and dialysis the next day. I would need to look for an apartment in the area while John was undergoing the scheduled procedures. I suddenly remembered that someone was coming to the house to install the chair lift for John. I signed a blank check and gave Ed the key to my front door. He agreed to go to the house and be there while the chair lift was being installed. Even though I was considering the possibility of apartment living for a short time, we would still find the chair lift useful for many months after John's surgery.

While John was having his scheduled treatments I was free to look at apartments. I had found one nearby with a short term lease that would even allow us to have pets. We could move our cats in with us which would be a great comfort to both of us while John waited for a liver. I had never experienced apartment living. This would be a new adventure for me and I was excited about it. Jimmy would move our few furniture items that would be necessary.

We would not need much, just our bed, a love seat and recliner and a small kitchen table with two chairs and a TV. We could survive with minimal dishes, pots and pans and wardrobe along with the few things our cats needed. I almost felt like a new bride setting up house for the first time. My first apartment!

The apartment manager was happy to meet me and eager to be of help. I paid her the application fee and filled out all the necessary forms. She would be in touch once the application was processed which would take a few days. I took some pictures of the beautiful new apartment. It was on a ground floor, no steps, and had a living room with a dining area, one bedroom, bath and kitchen. It was all that we needed, and elegant too. I was excited about showing John the pictures I had taken.

I returned to the hospital to find John finished with his procedure. He was feeling much more comfortable since seventeen liters of fluid had been drained from his belly. Perhaps he would have a restful night. I was not worried about dialysis which he would have tomorrow. We were in Hershey now, and each thing done was carefully monitored by the transplant team, which performed like a well oiled machine. We could relax knowing that John was in the best of care and all would be well.

Things were beginning to look very promising, especially when Jason came to tell us that there had been another offer for a liver. Dr. Schreibman was also a regular visitor along with his team of residents who were in the process of learning the art of medicine under his watchful eye. Priveleged were these young men and women who were learning from one of the best.

Once again we rode the roller coaster ride they call "waiting for a liver transplant." This time, it seemed, the climb to the top and subsequent dip were almost too much for John to bear. He became discouraged and depressed.

Perhaps I was being selfish asking him to hang on. He knew the Lord and we both knew where his eternal home would be. There would be no swollen belly there. No need for dialysis, or even a new liver. I pictured him as happy as he had looked as a little boy in his mother's picture books that she had kept year by year. She and his dad would be there to comfort him. He would run and jump and play. He would be happy and wait for me. "Do you want me to call hospice?" I asked him. "I don't know. Maybe." He answered.

The young female resident from Dr. Schreibman's team came to see us. "We were just talking about hospice" I explained. She knelt down to face John and in her gentle voice encouraged us both not to give up now. We had come so far. We both cried and agreed that she was right. The fight and the wait were on once again. John would be discharged and we would return for routine treatment three times a week while we waited for news of the apartment and new liver.

We arrived home to the new chair lift. It was wonderful and worked like a charm! Jimmy and John's friends were happy to see us and all had fun trying out the new ride on our staircase. I joked with them about putting a coffee can at the top to be used for ride fees. I could sell tickets for the rides like they do at an amusement park. I called Ed to tell him that we were home. He told me that I would find my blank check in the folder with the paperwork that came with the chair. Ed had paid for the chair and installation fee. He had wanted to do something nice for John. Always practical and thoughtful, that's Ed.

Twenty Four

Life was moving along. We were managing, and doing as well as expected under the circumstances. John was able to swallow and enjoy small portions of food. He drank his Ensure shakes, for which I was grateful. Some nutrition was making its way into his broken body. We could hang on and wait for that precious call.

I was grateful for these moments where we could just be together. John could sit in his recliner in the living room. I would give him his daily shave and sponge bath and comb his hair so that he could look and feel normal. We would talk or watch TV together just like in the old days when all was well.

John was doing so well today. He had eaten his small breakfast and it had stayed in his stomach. He tolerated his medicines well too and once again was able to enjoy the newspaper as his mind was clear. His medicines were working well and I was so happy for him. I knew he would be delighted to be having company later on today.

John's Knights Templar friends had contacted me and made arrangements to stop by. They had just returned from their annual convention and were in possession of John's Past Division Commander regalia for his uniform. They wanted to deliver it and personally congratulate him for completing his three year term. I was so glad they would find John in good spirits.

John decided to take an afternoon nap. I agreed it would be a good idea. That way he would be well rested when our company arrived later on. I helped him to the bedroom and tucked him into bed. I told him I would be in the front garden for a little while. The weeds were growing like crazy. He assured me he would be fine and I would check on him periodically.

I donned my garden gloves and began pulling weeds. My front yard was beginning to look like a residence again instead of a jungle. One of those weeds was so big I could have sworn it had roots to China. I positioned myself alongside the weed. It was me against the weed, and I was determined to win. I tugged and tugged until finally, SNAP! I won, but the force of gravity sent me tumbling forward, landing right on my face! The indignity! And my nose hurt too.

I whimpered, set aside the weed, and realized it was time to check on John anyway. I went into the house and found him peacefully sleeping. Then I looked in the bathroom mirror to check on my wounds. My nose was bleeding and I could feel a bruise forming at the bridge of my nose. By morning, who knows? Maybe I would be all black and blue and look like a raccoon. Poor me! I'm hurt and John is too sick to comfort me. I'm tired of being tough. I want to be babied again. Who will comfort me when I'm wounded?

I had my short pity party, after which I cleaned myself up. The Sir Knights would be here soon and John was having a good day. That's all that mattered in the moment.

John woke up and I helped him to get dressed. We made our way to the living room for another small meal and some relaxation. "Twenty Four is on tonight." John told me. "It's the two hour season finale." Twenty four had been John's favorite TV show. It's an espionage thriller about a counter terrorism team who saves the U.S.A. from almost certain disaster in a time span of twenty four hours. Every one hour episode ends with a cliff hanger ending, teasing the viewer to tune in for the next thrilling episode. I was enjoying this series with John. Tonight we would see the lead character, Jack Bauer, singlehandedly save our beloved country. We couldn't wait!

"Well, I have a surprise for you." I confessed. I had been trying to keep secret the fact that John was having company tonight. "We're having company. Al and Bob are coming. They want to bring your Past Division Commander cord and pin for your uniform." John was pleased. I once again combed his hair to make him look nice. "That's why I wanted you to look nice and be well rested today." I told him.

A short time later I heard cars pulling into the driveway. Al and Bob had arrived. So had Frank, and also, Jerry and his wife, Janet. Jerry had been elected to the Grand Line of Officers of the PA Grand Commandery. If all went as hoped for he would become the Grand Commander of PA Knights Templar in a few short years. I was friendly with Janet, who was a fellow officer in the Social Order Of Beauceant. I was happily surprised to see a few more familiar faces than were originally expected.

138

They all greeted John, who was equally happy to see them. They told him of how he had been missed at their convention and presented us with a gift basket of comforting goodies and snacks. They also presented us with a greeting card signed by the Sir Knights in attendance at convention, who had collected $200 for our current expenses. It brought tears to our eyes.

I retrieved John's Knights Templar uniform jacket from the bedroom and slipped it on him. He looked dwarfed in it. By now he had lost over 60 pounds to liver disease. We slipped the red cord onto the shoulder and positioned the new shoulder boards. The Past Division Commander pocket name tag was inserted in its proper place on the uniform. John stood as proudly as he was able as I took pictures of the momentous occasion. I quickly viewed the pictures I had taken and quietly gasped. I was literally staring death in the face. John had become so jaundiced and drawn. He looked like a neon green skeleton with piercing yellow eyes. I put on my best "poker face" and didn't react.

"Let's all pray." Jerry advised. We gathered in a circle and Jerry prayed. He prayed that on this very night a liver would become available for John. That it would be delivered quickly and would be a perfect match for John. Two hours later we were alerted to come to Hershey. Somewhere a thirty-six year old man had paid the ultimate price. Someone had to die so that John would have life. In a way, it was a gentle reminder that some two thousand years ago Someone had to die so that all who believe would have life, and have it abundantly. For John, there would be more Christmas Eve birthdays. There would be more opportunities to volunteer at the fire company. There would someday be a wedding, and a daughter-in-law, and perhaps, more grandchildren. There would even be a "liver-versary". All because somewhere a family gave that most precious gift imaginable; the Gift Of Life.

We said goodnight and the Sir Knights left. Just in time to tune in for the season finale of Twenty Four. John told me that he would not be taking any phone calls until after 10PM. He didn't want to miss a minute of Twenty Four. "Even if it's Hershey I'm not answering the phone." He informed me. Jokingly, I agreed as we settled in to enjoy the show.

One hour and 45 minutes later my cell phone rang. It was Hershey. "We would like you to come. We have an offer for a liver." The transplant coordinator on call informed me. "Who was that?" John asked. "Oh, it was Hershey." I answered, "Another 'hurry up and wait'. You're probably the back up again." I had told them we would arrive around midnight. We would take our time. "Let's finish watching Twenty Four." And we did.

Pleased that Jack Bauer had saved the U.S.A., I collected my usual belongings along with my "liver transplant Bible", the manual I had been given that contained all the necessary paperwork, and helped John to the car. Jimmy pulled into the driveway as we were leaving. "We're off to liver land." I told him. "Let's hope it's not another false alarm." It wasn't.

Finally . . . A New Liver

All was calm. Traffic was light as we drove to Hershey on what would be the momentous occasion in our lives. John was comfortable stretched out on the front passenger seat of my little PT Cruiser. We had adjusted the seat to a reclining position a few months ago to accommodate his swollen belly. John rested on his pillow and enjoyed the leisurely ride while I drove on.

True to my promise, we arrived at the main entrance to Hershey Medical Center around midnight. I pulled up to the entrance and helped John out of the car. I told him to select a wheelchair from the ample supply that had accumulated at the entrance while I found a place to park the car. I wheeled John inside the lobby and followed the procedure as I had been instructed to do for after hours check-in. The person on the other end of the phone advised me to take the main elevators to the 3rd floor.

Things were moving along now. Perhaps this night would provide what we had all been waiting for, a new liver, and now I was eager to get John into the doctors' and nurses' hands. Quickening my steps, I wheeled John along the long corridor that led to the main elevators. I noticed that he sounded out of breath. I stopped and looked down. "Why are you out of breath?" I asked. "I'm the one pushing the chair along." "I know." He answered, "but you're going too fast. I'm trying to keep up." I looked down at his feet and noticed that the wheelchair had no foot rests. John had been "running along", shuffling his feet, trying to keep up with my pace. Kind of like those cars that the Flintstones drive in the prehistoric cartoon. They hold the car up around their middle and run along with their feet because the wheel had not yet been invented. "Just hold your feet up." I told John. "You'll be so worn out you'll need a heart transplant by the time we get to the elevator!"

The elevator doors opened and I swung John's chair around and backed him in. By this time I had become a pro at maneuvering wheelchairs. The doors opened at the 3rd floor. We were greeted by a large sign that read "Welcome to 3rd floor. Obstetrics and Gynecology." A nurse stood at the entrance. "Uhh. I think we are in the wrong place." I smiled shyly. "Are you the Ellermanns?" She asked. "You're in the right place." She assured us. "Follow me. We're going to Same Day Surgery." "I didn't know they could do a liver transplant that quick!" I mumbled under my breath. The nurse laughed.

There were no beds available on the 5th floor where the transplant patients are usually admitted. Arrangements were made for John to be prepped in the same day surgery unit as he waited for surgery. A cot was brought in for me to sleep on. It wasn't my usual cot. It was wider but the springs in the middle had been stretched out, thus making it very uncomfortable to sleep on. I tried for a few hours, then folded it up and thanked the nurses for their kindness. I found a recliner that was much more comfortable.

Jason, the transplant resident doctor stopped by to give us an update. He was happy to see John and told us he hoped the liver would be a good match. It was rumored that it may be in either Pittsburgh or Philadelphia and the doctors would have to physically look at it to make sure it was in good condition for transplant. He would keep us informed periodically while the nurses prepped John for surgery. "John is the back up for this liver, isn't that right?" I asked Jason. "I haven't heard who the back up is. I'm really not sure." He answered. All was quiet and calm as we settled in for the long wait.

All of the same day surgery patients had gone home. John was the center of the attention of the three nurses on duty in that unit. They were happy and excited. They didn't often have the opportunity to prep someone for something as complicated as a liver transplant.

John was being treated as a celebrity. The nurses dutifully kept track of his vital signs and double checked all of the orders for cross matching of blood. Each time John was called in for a liver there were seventeen tubes of blood collected for cross matching. Everything is double and triple checked. Nothing is overlooked. Nurses phoned the transplant group to check on the latest progress and kept us informed with each phone call. No news yet. It's like waiting for a baby to be born.

Morning arrived and there was still no word of a liver. Arrangements were made for John to receive his regularly scheduled dialysis at the in-patient unit at the hospital. I would have a few hours to grab a bite to eat and stop at the chapel to pray. I looked for the young, nameless chaplain but he was nowhere to be found. I sat at the little rock garden in the center of the chapel and listened to the trickle of the water as I quietly prayed. All was beyond our control now. God was watching over us and directing every scene in this drama we call life. My job was to wait upon the Lord.

John returned from his dialysis treatment. He was calm despite the fact that there had still been no word of the status of the liver. I was calm too. I felt bad for John because he could have nothing to eat or drink in the event that he may be having surgery. Thank goodness his appetite was small. Perhaps he wouldn't miss the food and drink. He was tired and fell asleep. I took a nap too.

Dr. Kadry entered the room. "Well, Mr. Ellermann" she reported. "It looks like this liver is a good match. We will have to physically inspect it to make sure, but from the blood work and medical history it looks like a good match for you." "He's the back up for this liver, isn't that right?" I asked. "Oh, no." she answered, "This liver is for you!" We looked at each other and smiled. This was IT! Cautiously optimistic, we waited.

It was beginning to look more and more as if surgery was imminent. Kathy, the nurse came to make the final preparations. "We have to bathe you from head to toe" she instructed. I offered to help and began running the water in the sink to make it just the right temperature. Kathy placed a sheet on the floor and positioned a chair in the middle of the sheet. We helped John from the bed to the chair. I started at the top, washing his face, neck, arms and trunk while Kathy filled a small plastic basin with the warm water. She draped a towel over her forearm, placed the basin on the floor and knelt at John's feet. Gently, she began moistening his feet with the warm, soapy water. "Someone Else did this." She said in a gentle, angelic voice. "Someone Else did this. Do you know what I mean?" "Yes", John answered. "Our church has an Easter Musical every year and they once did a scene from that Scripture. "Let's pray." Kathy said, and we did. God was ready. The donor was ready. The doctors were ready, and we were ready. Dr. Kadry returned with the good news. Surgery was scheduled for 7:30AM.

Hershey Medical Center is a big, busy hospital. One would expect to hear traffic, footsteps, voices and other commotion but all remained calm. It was as if God had commanded the entire facility to become silent in reverent anticipation to await the miracle He was about to perform. Our world stood still to see His glory.

Some time ago I had dreamed of the day that John would receive his new liver. I hadn't thought much about it lately but I suddenly remembered that things were happening just as I had dreamed. The transport attendants came and wheeled John to the surgery area. I walked alongside the gurney and held his hand. He told me he wasn't afraid. Strangely, I wasn't either. All was calm as we approached the doors to the operating room. The attendants waited patiently while I kissed John and told him I would see him later.

Dr. Shah explained that the surgery would take about 8 hours. I could go to the surgical waiting area where I would be kept informed of the latest progress. It was there that the doctors would know where to find me if anything unexpected were to happen.

John told me later on that he was fascinated with the operating room. It was nothing like the kind you would see on TV. It was much smaller. All of the instruments were neatly lined up in readiness for use. There was a whiteboard on the wall containing a list of all the personnel who were scheduled for this procedure, beginning with the head surgeon right on down to every one of the nurses and technicians. There were many names on the board. The anesthesiologist explained some things to John and asked him if he had any questions. Then he told John to breathe deep and count backwards from 100. Ninety-nine, ninety eight, ninety seven—it felt like only fifteen minutes had passed as John was waking up from surgery. As Dr. Shah had promised, it had been eight hours.

I found the surgical waiting area. It was busy but the chairs were comfortable. There was the gift shop, Starbucks coffee shop and TV for the amusement of those waiting the outcome of their loved one's surgery. The nameless chaplain breezed through the area, smiling as he saw me. I recognized him right away. Same green shirt; same pink satin tie. I told him the good news that John was in surgery. He rejoiced, prayed with me and was on his way.

I began making phone calls and called our son, John. He told me that he would come and stay with me. Michelle would come too. I was happy that now I would have someone to sit with me. I gave my name at the reception desk. The receptionist gave me a slip of paper with a number on it. That number would appear on the TV screen on the wall. Instead of listing the patients by name, they were assigned case numbers. Listed alongside the case number was the status of that particular patient. It either read "patient in operating room", "patient in recovery area" or "patient assigned room."

John and Michelle arrived. We positioned ourselves near the screen and watched the number that had been assigned to John. It repeatedly read "patient in operating room". I sat for hours without taking my eyes off of the screen. I didn't want to miss a change in John's status. We made light conversation and played with our cell phones. I told the good news of John's surgery to each employee who recognized me. They were happy to hear the news. My son finally asked me, "Who are all these people?" I rattled off who they all were; the transport lady who had taken John for various tests, the nurses and technicians who took blood, one of the resident doctors, and even the man who emptied the wastebasket and brought John the morning paper every day. "Do you know everyone in this hospital?" John asked incredulously. "I guess I do." I answered. "We've been living here for a long time." Every one of these wonderful people genuinely cared about John, and me too.

The hours crept by. Ten thirty, eleven thirty, twelve thirty, and the case number still read "patient in operating room." I wondered how things were going. I had hoped to hear an update from one of the doctors, but no news yet. I asked the receptionist if there was any way we could be updated on John's status. "Oh, sure" she answered. "I can call the operating room nurse." I returned to my seat and waited. A few minutes later the receptionist came over to me and reported "They are putting the new liver in as we speak." 'My goodness!' I thought. 'He's been in there since 7:30AM. I hope they've kept it in a cooler. It'll be spoiled by the time they get it all hooked up.' A liver transplant is very complicated. It's much more than hooking up a few 'hoses' like they did with his open heart surgery.

Finally, around three thirty Dr. Uemura appeared in the surgical waiting area. He reported to us that all had gone well and I would be able to see John in about an hour. We all breathed a sigh of relief as I began making phone calls and sending text messages containing the good news. There were so many people to call.

John was assigned to a room in the surgical intensive care unit. There his vital signs and breathing would be monitored while he was in a drug induced coma for the next twenty four hours. I had become familiar with most of the machinery that he was hooked up to. We had been through much of this before when he had his open heart surgery.

I walked into the ICU area to look for John's room. Dr. Uemura sat at the nurses' station. He smiled broadly when he saw me. "I got the liver!" he exclaimed. "I put his name on it!" "You sure did!" I answered, and thanked him with tears in my eyes.

Our son, John, Michelle and I found John's room. His nurse was busy monitoring his vital signs and told us he was doing well. We were so happy to see him. Even though he was asleep she told us he would hear us if we talked to him. His color was pink. No more jaundice! We hadn't seen him like that in a long time. I leaned close and whispered in his ear, "Hi Hone! (That's what we had always called each other.) You got a new liver!" I had dreamed of this moment, and now our dream had come true.

Dr. Kadry came to the ICU to check on John's progress. "I'm glad we did this surgery." she told me in a pleasant, confident tone. "You know, it was your letter that did it. I looked at your letter and told the selection committee that we needed to take a closer look at this case." I was astonished! God had cleared my mind in one of my darkest hours to write boldly and passionately to convince the doctors to take a chance with John. Dr. Schreibman had heard the good news and came to see John too. He was so pleased that John had once again beaten the odds. I told them both, "I think we have all learned something here today." They looked at each other and shook their heads in agreement. "It was your faith." Dr. Kadry answered. Dr. Schreibman said "There is nothing like the determination of the human spirit." I am confident that in the future when these doctors are presented with a challenging case they will say to each other "Remember John Ellermann. Let's do this again." Somewhere a life will be saved. Only God knows who that person will be.

I would be able to sleep peacefully tonight even though I didn't have my cot. Cots were not permitted in the ICU waiting area, but there were two couches. One would have to do. I had found a supply of sheets, blankets and pillows in the hallway and I had a basin and toiletries from John's room on the 3rd floor. I could wash up in the restroom and sleep on the couch.

The nameless chaplain had encouraged me to fill out an application for a room at The Parsonage, a local house located next door to a nearby church. The Parsonage is kind of like a Ronald McDonald house for adults. There is a comfortable living room and dining room and a large kitchen where simple meals can be prepared. There are four bedrooms which can comfortably house a family of four. The house is equipped to furnish lodging for up to four families and is maintained by a ministry called Love, INC. (Love In the Name of Christ) Applications may be obtained through hospital social workers who have been assigned to transplant patients and their families.

I thanked the chaplain and told him I would be quite comfortable here in the waiting area. All of the other families had gone home for the night and I had the whole waiting area to myself. There were reading materials, TV and a computer where I could connect to the internet. There was a vending area where I could get snacks and beverages. The cafeteria on the main floor was open until 2AM and I could visit the chapel twenty four hours a day. I would be happy here. I would be close by to frequently check on John. This was where I wanted to be. The chaplain smiled, prayed with me and left.

I slept for a few hours at a time. I would check on John each time that I woke up. Each time I found him doing well. I looked forward to the day when we would be able to go home and begin our life with his new liver.

5-29-10

We're so happy to see
that you made it through
your surgery. We are
praying for you + your
family, + hope that you
will be home soon. From
the nurses that got you
ready, in Heart + Vascular
Out patient Care (HVOC)
May GOD bless you always,
Kathy, Lois + Penny
the Night Shift

Awake!

The following morning things were progressing even better than expected. I had thought that John would remain in his drug induced coma for at least two days. He was still connected to the respirator but he was wide awake and alert. He wanted to talk, but the nurses needed to wait for orders from Dr. Uemura before removing the breathing tube.

I talked to John and looked around the room. I found a clipboard with a diagram on it which showed pictures of the stages of liver disease. Dr. Uemura entered the room. He examined and talked with John, pleased with his progress. He would place an order for John's breathing tube to be removed. "Any questions?" he asked. John shook his head, yes. We gave John the clipboard and a paper and pen. He wrote "will I have a scar?" Dr. Uemura laughed and answered, "Yes, a big one. You have a whole new liver." I took the clipboard and showed Dr. Uemura the diagram of the diseased livers. "Which one of these did John's old liver look like?" I asked. He pointed to the worst looking one labeled necrotic cirrhosis. "This one." He answered. "This one here. Very bad liver!" I breathed a sigh of relief and silently thanked God and the donor family.

Today was turning out to be a wonderful day! Pastor Doug and his wife, Karen had arrived. They were very happy to hear the news and couldn't wait to see John. We made our way to John's room where we found the nurse and technician busy at work. They were preparing to remove John's breathing tube. The nurse instructed John to take a few deep breaths and exhale as the tube was being removed.

I leaned close and told John to breathe with me. I did as the nurse had instructed. Two deep breaths and blow, and out came the tube! "Praise the Lord!" John exclaimed. We were all overjoyed. John could breathe on his own, and he could even talk! We all thanked God and enjoyed our visit with our beloved pastoral family. I had so wished the nameless chaplain could be here to see this, but he was nowhere to be found. Perhaps I would find him on the 5th floor. John would be moved there soon.

Post Transplant

Once again, John, the celebrity had been assigned to the fifth floor. We rejoiced in seeing the familiar, friendly faces of the nurses and staff there. My cot had been delivered. I could room in next to John and learn how to take care of him at home now that he was post transplant.

John was a delightful patient for the nurses to tend to. He dutifully took his medicines and tried his best to do all that they wanted him to do. He didn't like the taste of Nystatin, a yellow liquid given at mealtimes. He was instructed to take a cupful and swish it around in his mouth a few times, then swallow. We called it the "swish and swallow". It tasted bad, but not as bad as the dreaded lactulose. There would be no more of that bad tasting syrupy liquid to help his liver function. The worst was behind us now.

John's appetite was improving as well. He was now able to eat things that he hadn't eaten in almost a year. We were all excited with each new baby step of progress that we could see. His friend, Frank from Knights Templar called faithfully every morning at 9AM for the daily update. John even talked to Frank each time he was awake. Frank posted the daily update of John's progress on the Facebook wall for all of his Masonic friends to see. Everyone was excited about John's recovery. There was even talk of John being discharged from the hospital in just a few short days. Dr. Uemura wanted John to stay at a short term rehab facility but I assured him that I could take care of him at home. After one bad experience in a short term rehab what John now needed was the comfort of his home and family. We would take good care of him and his new liver.

I listened intently as Velma, the social worker explained the details of John's new medications. I took detailed notes and took care of the financial arrangements for the medicines to be ordered. The $6,000 raised by the Trexlertown Fire Company would cover the cost.

Each day John was monitored, weighed, poked and prodded. The reports were all good. His liver function was excellent! Soon we would be going home!

Friends and family came to visit, and with each new day found John steadily improving. Frank came one night and we walked the length of the entire hallway. We sat at the end of the hallway and talked for awhile. Perhaps tomorrow we could visit in our own house, we told Frank.

I had decided to return home overnight to prepare the house for John's homecoming. I wanted everything to be clean. Clean bathroom, clean sheets and clean dishes to eat off of. What a treat it was to sleep in my own bed and be with my cats! I had missed them so, and I could tell that they had missed me too. I knew John would be safe in the care of the nurses on the 5th floor. His new liver was working fine. What could go wrong?

Almost Home . . . . Not!

I drove back to Hershey early in the morning. By now I had been able to make the trip practically with my eyes closed. The car seemed to be on "auto pilot" as I drove along enjoying the beautiful weather and scenery. It seemed as though the sun shone on Hershey every morning. I had experienced day after day of beautiful weather during our stay there. How I wished I lived near this place. I was beginning to feel so at home here. A few days earlier the apartment manager had called me with a move in date of June 11th. I thanked her and told her the good news of John's liver transplant. We would not be needing the apartment after all.

John was happy to see me. He had experienced a comfortable night but always felt better when I was there by his side. We went through our daily routine of medicines, food and grooming.

It was time for John's usual walk in the hallway. In the early days following his surgery he had used a walker. He would use it to walk to the lobby and walk back and forth at the elevators for a little extra exercise. We would often see Dr. Shah coming off the elevator. "It looks like a Roomba!" he would exclaim in an amused tone. "Maybe we could hook up a mini vacuum cleaner to that walker and clean the floors at the same time." I told him I would consider that when we returned home.

John wanted to try walking without using the walker for this trip. I agreed to try. I would wheel his IV pole alongside of him and he could use it for support. We made our way to the hallway and I discovered that it was impossible to wheel an IV pole in a straight line without steering with both hands. That wouldn't work for John. I agreed to steer the pole while he walked.

We walked a short distance in the hallway when we reached a computerized scale with a "do not touch" sign on it. The scale had been set and would lose its accuracy if it were touched. Two nurses stood nearby and were carrying on a conversation with each other. "I hope nobody touches that scale." I heard one of them say. "Yeah." I said. "I see it says 'do not touch'". John stood still and put his hand on the scale. That was odd! Completely out of character for John. He would never have deliberately touched it. "Are you tired?" I asked him. There must be some logical explanation, I thought. He answered "yes" and I saw a wheelchair at the end of the hallway. The nurses stayed with him while I went to retrieve it.

We positioned John in the wheelchair. Perhaps I would take him for a ride instead of a walk. As I stood talking to the nurses, all of a sudden John cried out. "Ahh!" He brought his hands to his head, and at the same time his eyes rolled up in his head. His body went stiff and convulsed wildly, then he went limp, losing consciousness.

I stood there in shock. The nurses pushed the wheelchair backward all the way to his room while resident doctors and more nurses appeared with a crash cart. One of the nurses stayed with me outside the room and summoned a female chaplain who had been visiting someone else on the floor. They escorted me to the nurses' desk. The chaplain talked to me but I don't remember what she was saying. I kept looking down the hallway for any telltale activity going on in John's room. What had just happened? We had come so far, for this? Would I be returning home alone as I had feared?

Soon a nurse came to give us an update. John had experienced a seizure. Sometimes this happens as a result of the anti-rejection medicine, Prograf. John just happened to be one of the people who would experience a side effect from it.

I was escorted by the nurse back to John's room. He was awake and alert, thank God. He recognized me and knew where he was, but remembered nothing of the seizure. Jason, the transplant resident stood by John's bedside and asked him questions. He asked him to stick out his tongue, move his eyes and smile. "Did he always have a slight droop on one side of his smile?" Jason asked. In thirty three years of marriage I had never noticed a droop when John smiled. It was so slight that only the trained eye of a physician would notice it.

The doctors had a hunch that Prograf was the culprit that had caused the seizure but they wanted to make sure nothing else was going on. John would need to be moved to ICU and monitored closely for 48 hours. During that time tests would be done to make sure there was no damage to his brain. We would not be going home after all.

Let's Try This Again

John was poked and prodded, tested and re-tested by a very sweet, compassionate young lady named Dr. Bernard. There were no signs of brain damage or stroke. A technician wheeled machinery into his room and prepared the machinery while an assistant placed electrodes on John's scalp. "How about that!" I exclaimed to the technician. "All those brain waves and no 'bzzzt thing!" We all laughed as we remembered lines from one of our favorite comedy movies, "The Man With Two Brains." It was a sci-fi spoof that John and I had watched many times. The technician had seen the movie too and joked along with us.

Dr. Shah came to see John. He was surprised to hear that John was back in the ICU. "What happened?" he asked. I explained that John had experienced a seizure from Prograf. "Do you remember it?" Dr. Shah asked. "No. He doesn't." I answered, "but I do." "What did it look like?" Dr. Shah wanted to know.

I told Dr. Shah I would show him. He smiled and explained to John, "This is called method acting." "Watch this" I instructed as I pulled up a chair. I sat in the chair and acted out John's seizure exactly as I had witnessed it. "That's a seizure, all right!" exclaimed Dr. Shah. He then gave us the good news that the brain wave test showed all normal activity and gave the order for John to be returned to the fifth floor. He would be placed on a different anti-rejection medication. The doctors would add anti seizure medication too as a precaution so this would not happen again.

We returned to the fifth floor later that day. John was comfortable and so was I. My cot was positioned alongside of John's bed and my belongings were tucked away in the night table. I checked my e-mail and facebook wall on my laptop computer while John watched TV. We could live like this for a few more days. Hopefully we would be going home soon.

Internal Bleeding

Each day we continued the routine of daily hospital life. John's blood was tested for abnormalities in his liver function. All was well, liver wise. He was given his daily medications and continued to be aggressively treated with blood thinner medication since a blood clot had been found in his portal vein during transplant surgery. The doctors were not about to take any chances with a blood clot. John walked each day as he had been instructed and wore what we called his "purr-purr boots" while in bed. They consisted of two wrap around "socks" that were placed on his legs and hooked up to a bedside motor that pumped air into the socks. The socks rhythmically inflated and deflated thus keeping the blood circulating in his legs. The sound they made reminded us of our cats purring. We looked forward to being at home once again with our family and cats.

John woke at 3AM and wanted to walk to the bathroom. I disconnected the purr-purr boots and helped him to his feet. I had become very familiar with this equipment and how to operate it. As I tucked John back into bed he told me that he felt completely worn out, very weak. Perhaps his blood sugar was low. I called the nurse to come and check his vital signs. They seemed to be ok. The nurse thought that perhaps he was having a panic attack. That was possible after all he had been through. The nurse told me she would note all of this on John's chart and he would be checked again at 6AM.

Like clockwork, the nurses and residents arrived at 6AM to check on John. We had both tried to sleep for a little while between 3 and 6. They turned on the light and I thought, 'he looks pale.' The residents thought so too. They ordered the usual blood work. The nurse helped John to a sitting position while the digital scale was brought into the room to check his daily weight. We helped John to stand. He took two steps toward the scale and passed out backward onto the bed. 'Another seizure?' I thought. 'How can this be?'

One of the resident doctors returned to the room with the results of John's blood work. "His platelets are very low." He announced. "We need a CT scan to see if there is bleeding anywhere." John would be moved to ICU again on the second floor. I began to pack my belongings as Jason wheeled the bed with John in it out of the room. Two nurses came to the room to report that they had called for transport. They asked, "Where did they go?" "Second floor." I answered. "For a scan or something." They looked at each other bewildered. "Who took him?" one of them asked. "Jason. Why?" I answered. "They never do transport themselves unless it's really urgent." One of them told me. I quickly left the room and dashed to the south elevator, leaving the two bewildered nurses behind.

I arrived at the ICU waiting room and quickly dumped my belongings in an area I would claim as my new home for as long as needed. Then I went to find John. He was on his way to the operating room. Doctors and nurses surrounded his gurney as Dr. Shah quickly trailed along behind. "Will he be ok?" I called out. Dr. Shah spun around to face me. "We will do all we can." He said. "We found internal bleeding somewhere but we don't know exactly where it's coming from. I'll come and give you the details as soon as I'm done."

I stood by and helplessly watched as my best friend of thirty some odd years disappeared behind the operating room doors. Perhaps this would be the last I would see of John. Would I be returning home a widow? Dazed, I returned to the waiting area to await further news of John's fate and my future.

The nameless chaplain stood in the waiting area. He smiled that same gentle smile when he saw me. How I missed Jimmy! "How is John, the Beloved?" he asked in his usual gentle tone. "John, the Beloved has had a setback." I explained. "There's internal bleeding someplace. They are in the operating room now trying to find out where it's coming from." "The doctors will find it." He assured me.

"You need to get some rest. You really ought to consider going to The Parsonage." He encouraged. "I'll be ok here." I explained. "There is a couch. I have blankets and pillows, and it gets quiet when everyone else goes home." I looked around the room sadly. 'This will have to do until he comes out of surgery.' I thought. The chaplain prayed with me and then disappeared down the hallway. I suddenly felt exhausted. Perhaps I would follow through on his idea about The Parsonage once John was in recovery.

Four hours later Dr. Shah found me in the waiting area. He reported that there was internal bleeding into John's abdominal cavity but it was not anything the doctors could stitch. It was more of an abrasion where they had cut the old liver away from the abdominal wall. The fact that John had been treated aggressively with blood thinners following transplant had only made this bleeding more profuse. The plan was to stop the aggressive blood thinner treatment and give John blood products to replace the blood he had lost to improve clotting factors. This would take a couple of days. I would be able to see John as soon as he was in recovery, which I hoped would be soon.

I made some phone calls, updating family and friends about the latest findings, then made my way to the recovery area in the ICU. John lay once again in a drug induced coma oblivious to all of the machinery around him. The technician monitored the breathing machine and showed me the two different colors of lines on the graph. One represented the machine's breath, the other, John's. I was encouraged to see that he was breathing on his own. Bag after bag of blood products were hooked up to the IV pole as the life giving substance flowed into John's veins. I watched as the nurses emptied the plastic bulbs at the ends of the drains that had been inserted into John's abdomen. I whispered into John's ear that he was out of surgery and the doctors and nurses were watching him carefully. God was watching over us as well. I told him that the nameless chaplain had asked about him and prayed for us. John's eyelids fluttered as I spoke. There was nothing else I would be able to do for him at the moment.

I went to the nurses' station where I found Dr. Shah. I thanked him for his quick thinking and skill as a surgeon. "I really am feeling very tired." I told him. "I think maybe

I will try to get a room at The Parsonage." "That would be a good idea." He answered. "Just make sure we have your cell phone number. John will be ok. If anything happens, you will be the second person to know. I will be the first." He assured me.

I retreated to the waiting area and called Velma, the social worker. I told her that I would like an application for a room at The Parsonage. "That's a good idea." She said cheerfully. "I'll bring you one shortly." "Ok." I answered. "I'll be in the ICU waiting area." Then I plopped into a chair, put my feet up on a matching ottoman and fell sound asleep.

I woke up just as Dr. Shah was walking through the waiting area. "I thought you were going somewhere to get some sleep." He exclaimed as he saw me. "I am. I'm going to The Parsonage. I called Velma and she's bringing me an application for a room there." I answered in a sleepy tone. Dr. Shah knelt down to meet me at eye level and scolded, "If you don't go somewhere and get some sleep you're gonna wind up being a patient here too and I don't want to take care of two of you!" "I know." I answered, more wide awake now. "I'm going!" He then called Velma, who appeared moments later with my application. She had been there earlier but noticed that I was asleep and she didn't want to disturb me.

The Parsonage . . . . And The Angel

John rested comfortably and was monitored constantly in the ICU. I sat at his bedside for awhile as he slept and woke for brief periods. I explained to him that I would be at The Parsonage during the night, which was only about five minutes away. The nurses and doctors had my cell phone number if they needed to update me on his condition. I promised John that I would be back early in the morning. He nodded "ok" and went back to sleep. I tiptoed out of the room and returned to the waiting area where I collected my belongings.

Application in hand I found my way to The Parsonage. I turned onto the street that led to the Spring Creek Church of the Bretheren which stood on a cul de sac next door to the building. The neighborhood was beautiful! The houses were equally attractive. Each one was framed by a beautifully manicured lawn with decorative bushes and flower beds. The street was lined with old fashioned streetlamps which added to the quaintness of this neighborhood. It reminded me of summers spent years ago in the quiet, beautiful place where my grandparents had lived. If only the nameless chaplain could see how comforting this setting was to me.

The Parsonage volunteer greeted me with encouragement and enthusiasm. She looked over my application and showed me around, helping me to get acquainted. She showed me the pantry which had been stacked with non perishable foods and assigned an area in the refrigerator where I could store anything perishable that I wished to buy. "Oh, look." She exclaimed. "Someone left a half gallon of milk and it's still usable. Must have been the people who checked out yesterday. You can use it if you want." Tomorrow morning I would be able to have a bowl of cereal here instead of spending money in the cafeteria.

The volunteer gave me a room and house key and explained that I could come and go as I pleased. Each room had it's own supply of linens which were used during the stay and then placed in the laundry basket on the floor in the bedroom closet. Volunteers would collect the linens at the end of a guest's stay, do the laundry and return with the clean linens for the next guest.

My room had two full size beds. Atop the dresser stood a small basket filled with necessary items such as soap, shampoo, conditioner, toothpaste, toothbrush and mouthwash. I unpacked my belongings. At last I could find my clothes from a drawer now instead of rooting through the wrinkled mess in a duffel bag. There was even an iron so that I could freshen up my clothes.

I slept soundly that evening. I awoke a few times to the sounds of the other guests as they quietly climbed the stairs and made their way to their rooms. I wondered about them. What crisis were they facing in their lives? Perhaps I would meet some of them tomorrow night.

Early the next morning I woke up refreshed and looked at the clock. 6AM. I quickly showered and dressed and enjoyed a bowl of cereal in the quaint dining room. I wanted to be at the hospital in time for the doctors to make their rounds so that I would be kept informed of the latest news of John's condition. I also wanted to find the chaplain and tell him that I had taken his advice and was enjoying my stay at The Parsonage.

John was doing as well as could be expected. The doctors wanted to keep the breathing apparatus in place just in case they needed to open him up again in the event of more internal bleeding. I had hoped not. When they did the last surgery they had to open his entire transplant incision which included removing 64 staples and then stitch it all back up when they were finished.

The bulbs at the end of John's drains were filled with red liquid. The nurse told me the liquid was a lighter color than it had been the day before which meant that the bleeding was slowing down somewhat. She emptied the liquid into a container that resembled a large measuring cup. The bulbs refilled rather quickly so I emptied them when I saw that they were full. I recorded the time on a piece of paper and left the liquid in the measuring cup for her to see. She appreciated this and was happy that I helped. It gave me something to do while I sat with John.

When John would fall asleep I would slip off to the waiting area where I had met some new friends. There were many opportunities to talk and pray with people as we were all in the same boat, so to speak. I looked forward to hearing the latest news of their loved one's progress and prayed with them. Some of the people who had not yet heard about John thought I worked there. I was beginning to look and feel as though I belonged here. "I don't work here." I would often joke, "I just live here."

I visited the chapel and wrote prayer requests for the people I had met in the ICU waiting area. The dimly lit, quiet chapel was a good place for prayer and reflection. I had been there several times since John's surgery in search of the nameless chaplain. I had even inquired of him to the receptionists and other chaplains. No one had heard of him. I wished I could remember his name. I couldn't, but gave each one I spoke with a detailed description of him. He just didn't sound familiar to anyone. We never saw him again.

The Bible advises us that we may entertain angels without having any knowledge of it and I believe that's exactly what happened in this case. There is just no other explanation for it. Months later we were shown pictures of the hospital chaplains by the pastor at the Spring Creek Church of the Bretheren. We recognized some of the other chaplains but there was no sign of this particular chaplain in the pictures. We had been touched by an angel.

I returned to The Parsonage each evening with renewed strength and hope to face the next day. I met a lady whose daughter was in the ICU waiting for a heart transplant. This lady had been a heart transplant recipient herself a handful of years ago due to a genetic default in her heart. Her two daughters suffered from the same condition. She would soon need to experience the transplant process with her second daughter, who remained symptom free at present. And I thought I had it bad! It's amazing what some people endure. I told her of John's condition and we prayed together. We enjoyed some conversation and then headed off to bed.

The Parsonage volunteer visited us in the hospital as promised. By this time John had been moved to the fifth floor with hopes of going home in a few days. The volunteer introduced me to another family whose loved one was awaiting a liver transplant. They were from our area too. I looked forward to the process of getting to know them but was not able to since their loved one was being discharged to a short term rehab to await liver transplant. I felt a special bond with these people. We were kindered spirits.

John's drain bulbs were changing in color of liquid. The liquid now appeared as kool aid and wasn't nearly as dark as before. This was a very good sign! A few more days passed and the drains were emptied less and less until they were finally removed. We rejoiced; I attended Spring Creek Church on Sunday and looked forward to returning home. The people at Spring Creek Church rejoiced with me, and the pastor had even offered to visit with John. This particular Sunday was the pastor's birthday and a birthday cake had been provided for him. I didn't want to take him away from his celebration. I thought at that particular time that perhaps the nameless chaplain would show up somewhere on the 5th floor at the hospital, but as previously mentioned, we never saw him again.

On June 14th we were given the good news that John would be discharged tomorrow. At last, we were going home! I returned to The Parsonage for what would be the final night of my stay. I calmly and confidently entered the living room and sat on the couch.

I smiled at the frail, thin middle aged man who sat flipping through magazines in the easy chair across from me. "How long have you been staying here?" I asked. "My husband had a liver transplant and we're going home tomorrow." I reported happily. "Oh, I'm a regular here." He explained. "I have lymphoma and am being treated with an experimental treatment by these amazing doctors at Hershey. I stay here Monday through Friday and get treated on an outpatient basis. Then I go home to upstate New York on weekends to be with my family. I have a teenage son there." We spoke some more and our conversation turned to spiritual things. "You know," he said. "Some people say they want to leave things in God's hands and they do just that, but then they don't do anything else. They expect God to handle everything." "That's true." I answered. "It's our job to make use of the technology God has provided us with and above all, put our faith in Him. All we need is that little bit of faith. You know what it says in the Bible. If you have faith as small as a mustard seed you can move a mountain." I stopped in mid sentence. "MY GOD!" I exclaimed. "I moved a mountain." "You sure did!" he laughed. "You sure did!"

Home . . . And Normal At Last!

John was discharged the following morning as promised. I had made detailed notes about his medicines and signs of rejection. He would need to return to Hershey once a week for his clinic appointments and have blood work done at St. Luke's twice a week.

We were excited about John's first post-transplant clinic visit, a real milestone! I parked the car and helped John into the building. We had come full circle now. We were here in the same place where we had first met Dr. Kadry and Dr. Schreibman. Wouldn't they be proud to see John now?

John approached the receptionist's desk with a renewed sense of confidence. The receptionist smiled up at him and asked, "Return liver?" "No thanks!" John replied. "This one is working just fine. I think I'll keep it." We all shared a good laugh.

The blood work became less frequent, as did the clinic visits over the next handful of months. Our new routine was becoming a way of life as we settled in. The first year was met with a few complications; one being the hernia repair which Dr. Shah would have preferred to wait a little longer for. The other was a case of high potassium which we now refer to as the "much ado about nothing" episode.

John is doing well and continues to improve. As I write this we are on our way to our trailer which is parked at a camping resort here in Northeastern PA. The sun is setting in the most beautiful blue sky I have ever seen. It is as if God has taken a paintbrush and painted an incredible sunset with the most beautiful array of color for us to enjoy as we dine on our deck and reflect on all that has happened in the past year.

Next week John will "graduate" as he sees the transplant surgeons for his last visit with them. He will then see Drs. Schreibman and Riley twice a year for routine checks, and will continue to take anti rejection medicine for the rest of his life.

LIFE. There's that word again! How do you say thank you to all those who saw to it that John has a second chance at life? I am so taken aback I can hardly write these words.

To the nurses and technicians who took such good care of John I would say you have certainly gone above and beyond the call of duty. To the doctors I would say the same, and I would add that while you were performing your dedicated skills things were going on around you that you were completely unaware of, and they were all good! (See the many references to the nameless chaplain mentioned several times throughout the story) To the many volunteers, family and friends who touched our lives in time of crisis I say thank you. Your dedication has made a great difference. To the prayer partners at Trinity Wesleyan Church, and especially to Pastor Doug, thank you ever so much for your prayers. God has heard our cries and performed a miracle for us to enjoy and to tell the world about.

Most importantly, there remains a nameless donor and his family, who chose to give that most precious gift in the hope of helping someone who they may never have the opportunity to meet. May they be forever blessed by their generosity and kindness. If you, the reader have never thought of having that "organ donor" inscription placed on your driver's license I would encourage you to do so now.

To the reader I would say I hope you have enjoyed our story. Perhaps you have been overcome with joy or wept in sadness. It is my profound prayer that as you read this you will believe, and have faith. All it takes is faith as small as a mustard seed and you too can move a mountain. We did.

Index of pictures:

Epilogue

Now that you have finished reading this book, we pray that your new understanding of this disease, the subsequent months, and our feelings will touch your lives too.

This is a story unfinished. In our lives there are many more chapters left to be written, thanks to John's liver donor family, the continuing care of the medical professionals, and the un-ending love of God. We are forever indebted to all of them.

About The Author

Jackie Ellermann has experienced first hand the challenges of caring for her husband, John through a devastating illness, and the joy of his subsequent recovery.

Born and raised in Kearny, NJ, Jackie has been married to John for 34 years. She is a retired administrative assistant who has held many leadership roles. Those include scouting, Order of the Eastern Star of NJ, Ladies Auxiliary of Knights Templar, PA, and Social Order of Beauceant.

Jackie has volunteered with Yokefellow Prison Ministry where she ministered to incarcerated youth for ten years. She is a member of Trinity Wesleyan Church, Allentown, PA.

Jackie resides in Allentown, PA with her husband, John and twin sons.

Made in the USA
Lexington, KY
08 December 2018